Redacted

# PRAISE FOR *REDACTED*

"*Redacted* is a must-read for anyone looking to learn about deliverance. The Church history on this topic is very interesting, and David does an incredible job laying it all out. *Redacted* gives some great insight into many questions, even some questions you may not have even known that you had. You'll be truly glad you read it!"
**—MASON LEDBETTER,** Author and HFD Ministries Lead

"*Redacted* takes you on a trip down memory lane that you never knew existed, and it truly lives up to its name *The Secret History of Deliverance and Exorcism.* I can say without a doubt that Miller truly took the time to make sure that this work was done with tremendous quality. *Redacted* will open your eyes to the unsettling reality that we are soldiers in a spiritual war and it's time to fight."
**—JASON RODRIGUEZ,** M.Div.

"*Redacted* is answered prayer for every believer. Someone has to write about this ministry and wake up the sleeping Church."
**—CHARLES COSTELLO,** Pastor of Ministry of Salvation Fellowship

"Miller provides compelling historical evidence to the reader that God has always had a remnant setting the captives free."
**—JOHN GOGUEN,** Th.M., Pastor of Agape Bible Fellowship

"*Redacted* is a fascinating exploration into the mystical and often misunderstood realm of exorcism and spiritual deliverance. With a meticulously researched narrative, Miller provides a comprehensive chronicle of the rituals, practices, and histories associated with expelling malevolent spirits from individuals and spaces. What sets *Redacted* apart is Miller's adept blending of historical accounts with socio-cultural analysis. One of the strengths of *Redacted* is its impartiality. Interspersed with personal accounts and testimonials, *Redacted* offers a humanizing touch to an often-feared topic. For those curious about the history and sociological implications of exorcism, *Redacted* serves as a valuable and enlightening resource."

—**BARRY COOK**, D.Min., Church Planter and
Author of *Mission Minded Leaders*

"Wow, *Redacted* is incredible, and it's a great way of both breaking down the history of deliverance for the average Christian's understanding, as well as a deep dive into the history of exorcism and deliverance in the Christian faith in general, and especially in the American church! I will say on a personal note as a pastor for twenty years, I see American Christians with a great need for deliverance. Many suffer from sickness, addictions, torment, suicidal thoughts, depression, anger and much more. I have to say about David himself, he adds a completely different perspective, not because of his research and hunger only, but because he, unlike most theologians, spent hundreds of hours not in study only but hundreds of hours in application as well! I would encourage any pastor, scholar, teacher, theologian, philosopher, or Christian leader, in the same thing that the apostle James encourages us, don't just be a hearer of this word, but be a Mark 16 and Luke 10 doer of the word! Read this work and go cast out demons! Go set sons and daughters free just like the Son of God came to do!"

—**BENJAMIN WISAN**, Pastor of Church Tsidkenu

# DAVID M. MILLER

# REDACTED

## The Secret History of
## Exorcism

NASHVILLE

NEW YORK • LONDON • MELBOURNE • VANCOUVER

# Redacted

## The Secret History of Exorcism

Published in New York, New York, by Morgan James Publishing. Morgan James is a trademark of Morgan James, LLC. www.MorganJamesPublishing.com

Proudly distributed by Publishers Group West®

**Morgan James BOGO™**

A **FREE** ebook edition is available for you or a friend with the purchase of this print book.

CLEARLY SIGN YOUR NAME ABOVE

**Instructions to claim your free ebook edition:**
1. Visit MorganJamesBOGO.com
2. Sign your name CLEARLY in the space above
3. Complete the form and submit a photo of this entire page
4. You or your friend can download the ebook to your preferred device

ISBN 9781636983301 paperback
ISBN 9781636983318 ebook
Library of Congress Control Number:
2023946398

**Cover & Interior Design by:**
Christopher Kirk
www.GFSstudio.com

Morgan James PUBLISHING

**Builds**

with...

**Habitat for Humanity®**
Peninsula and
Greater Williamsburg

Morgan James is a proud partner of Habitat for Humanity Peninsula and Greater Williamsburg. Partners in building since 2006.

Get involved today! Visit: www.morgan-james-publishing.com/giving-back

# TABLE OF CONTENTS

Chapter 6:
## THE PROTESTANT REFORMATION:
Exorcism Restored And Redacted
AD 1517–1700
103

Chapter 7:
## REASON AND REVIVALISM:
The Birth Of Evangelicalism
AD 1700–1900
123

Chapter 8:
## PENTECOSTALISM:
Unchecked Spiritual Power
AD 1880–1950
135

Chapter 9:
## THE RESTORATION OF HEALING AND DELIVERANCE:
The Old Guard
AD 1950–2000
159

Chapter 10:
## CONCLUSIONS: REVIVE OR REDACT?
187

# FOREWORD

Pastor Win Worley was my grandfather; I grew up at his church during this incredible time. I personally witnessed countless demonic manifestations, supernatural miracles, and healings. Thousands of people flocked year-round for healing, deliverance, and to learn how to cast out demons themselves. He dedicated his entire life to the Full Gospel of the Lord Jesus Christ and was a pioneer of the rediscovery of deliverance ministry. He wrote a series of books and booklets on deliverance and spiritual warfare; his last book, *Harassing the Hosts of Hell*, was dedicated to the next generation of deliverance workers. He believed that those who surrender to God will see and experience revival power, which has been hidden for centuries.

Still the debate of validity to modern-day exorcism continues while even more so, deliverance is rising to the forefront of Christianity. To know where we are going, we must know where we have been. When David Miller first got in touch with me, I was apprehensive about being interviewed and suggested some others to seek out first. I got to know David over the next two years, and it did not take long to see he was following the scripture; his methods and school of thought were in order, and he was walking the walk. I have seen him evangelize, preach, teach, and cast out devils, in the streets, in houses, and in churches.

When David first showed me *Redacted*, I realized that he was really writing the history of spiritual warfare. I found it fascinating as I had never read anything like it before. It was not written as opinion or as an instruction for or against a school of thought, but simply as an unredacted history of deliverance. I recommend *Redacted* to anyone looking into the historical nature of deliverance and spiritual warfare.

Brother Jason Worley

# PREFACE

C. S. Lewis once said that we should all read old books. Why? Because we are all beholden to biases, influences, and standards of thinking in our current culture and age, both their strengths and fallacies. By reading books from various periods, we expose ourselves to thinking not beholden to the same weaknesses of our own age. Those other ages had their own strengths and weaknesses, but they serve to challenge and balance our ways of thinking.

Today, Western evangelical Christianity has found itself in its own theological and cultural vacuum. We have our axioms. We repeat them in smooth phrases from the pulpit, make videos about them, put them on T-shirts, and shun any heretical influence that may say otherwise. This writing aims to expose my readers to the lives, theology, and ministry of other notable Christians throughout the great history of the Church, challenging some of our theological assumptions as it relates to deliverance and spiritual warfare.

Deliverance ministry has come to the fore more significantly in the last two years. The premise that many Christians are influenced by demons that drive them into sin, sickness, insanity, character flaws, etc., and that they need deliverance through exorcism is an unpopular and uncomfortable thought to most evangelical Christians in the West. It seems unbiblical, unorthodox, and novel. However, you will find here that this concept is neither new nor fringed in theology.

This work began as a small research essay for a writing class of mine at Regent University. I choose to write on the subject, especially exorcism in the early Church, Reformation, and Pentecostal eras. What I found out during that short project astounded me. The commonality of exorcism and its incredible resistance throughout the history I researched was incredible, so I kept researching and discovering more. The same pattern was repeated: revival, deliverance, redaction, and collapse.

To be forward, I am an advocate of contemporary deliverance ministry. However, my goal for this book was not to preach deliverance but to provide an objective, non-biased examination of history, which speaks for itself. In this reading, I ask you to set aside your presumptions and thoughtfully consider what Christians throughout Church history have thought and done on this subject.

# INTRODUCTION

I n the last several years, especially the last several months, deliverance ministry has become a frequent point of discussion and contention in the Church. Deliverance proponents believe that this is the continuation of Jesus's commands in Matthew 10:1 and Mark 16:17, and these orders are binding on Christians today. They believe that demons have remained largely hidden and unchallenged in the Church, as this practice has fallen out of use, and today, they hide under the surface, causing problems such as sickness, mental illness, addiction, and habitual sin. We could see incredible results if the Church would rise to the occasion and cast out demons. Many have gone through such deliverance and report receiving partial or full freedom from the issues they sought to alleviate.

However, this is unscriptural for most protestants, and numerous arguments advanced. For those of liberal theology, demons and devils don't exist at all. References to them in the Bible are simply divine accommodations for the ignorance of the day; the demons were mental disorders that Jesus healed, like other diseases, calling it demonic so it would make sense to his original audience.

Those of a Reformed theology believe demons do exist but that there is never a need to exorcise them. Casting out demons is a miracle, like healing, and all miracles, with some rare exceptions, stopped after the apostolic age and the completion of the New Testament. Demons may indwell unbelievers, but you cannot exorcise them because it would be useless. Instead, leading them to the saving grace of Christ will immediately deliver them. Since this automatically exempts Christians from the possibility of demonization, exorcising unbelievers is either impossible or unethical.

For Pentecostals and charismatics, the primary objection is that a demon cannot indwell Christians because of the presence of the Holy Spirit. Some would allow the possibility of a believer who is not baptized in the Holy Spirit to have a demon. Either way, the reasoning is that the Holy Spirit and the demon cannot dwell in the same space, and therefore, a Christian cannot have a demon. These Pentecostals may be more willing to cast demons out of unbelievers or defer to missionaries and their exorcisms in distant lands.

Another group objects because these problems are not demonic but come from having a lack of faith, not knowing one's identity, or not having proper spiritual health. For this teaching, to accept the possibility of demonization is to lack faith in Christ; those who go to deliverance ministry are going to a man and not to God, lacking trust and faith in Jesus. All these supposedly demonic problems are really the flesh nature that needs to be crucified and renewed.

Some believe in casting out demons in some way but criticize deliverance ministries for their seemingly complicated methods when Jesus apparently cast demons out with a word. Others say that demons are used as an excuse and deliverance as a panacea for people to ignore the process of sanctification. Needless to say, people have many objections to deliverance.

Despite these strong and well-entrenched criticisms, deliverance ministries continue to pop up and grow in popularity. More deliverance ministries, more videos about casting out demons, a stronger push to bring this type of ministry back to the front, and even a movie about deliverance ministry are all bucking the trend.

This debate about the legitimacy of deliverance ministry has occurred in the echo chamber of Western, twenty-first-century Christianity. Western, twenty-first-century protestants take issue with deliverance ministry, yes. But what about Christians in every other century and part of the world? Did they have anything to weigh in on the matter? Church history is *not* the authority of theology; it is a good litmus test of our biases and blind spots to the scripture. We all read with our own personal hermeneutic that our culture, mentors, and lives have influenced us with. Yet, this little personal view of the Bible isn't always right. Seeing how others understood the scripture who had different lenses is an important sounding board for orthodoxy.

This writing seeks to examine the thoughts and teachings throughout Church history on matters of spiritual warfare. How was warfare waged against Satan, if at all? For this writing, I will use the term "exorcism" to describe any kind of activity that seeks to expel demons, as opposed to deliverance. Though I personally prefer the latter, it is vague, especially when dealing with history. Further, I will use the term "demonized" to describe persons under the power of demons. Possession and oppression are misleading terms not present in Biblical Greek when it comes to demons, so I will generally avoid them unless they are used by an author we are examining.

Exorcism will be the primary focus of this examination, though we will highlight other concepts of spiritual warfare when appropriate. The legitimacy of contemporary deliverance ministry is challenged on several fronts, so we will examine several questions at the conclusion of each chapter to best understand our survey of Church history:

1. What context was exorcism used in? In other words, what was its purpose, and what problems did it seek to solve?

2. Who was casting out demons? Was there an "exorcist" office, or did pastors, or even laity, cast out demons? How common was it?

3. Since it is one of the most heated questions of today, were those exorcised Christians or unbelievers? What was the theology concerning the demonization of Christians?

4. For persons and times when exorcism was not written about/practiced, why? What were the theological, social, or other factors that led to this?

5. How was exorcism practiced? What method was used, and what did it look like?

6. How was spiritual warfare understood as a whole, exorcism or otherwise?

7. What factors drove changes in all the above throughout history?

8. Was this beneficial to the Church?

# CHAPTER 1

## THE FALL OF MAN

In the beginning, we know that God created the world and man to live in paradise, in perfect union with God, in peace and without bondage or affliction. God created Eden to be a colony of heaven, so to speak, and Adam was the provincial governor of the earth. In Genesis 1:27–30, God gave Adam the dominion mandate, giving him governmental power over the earth and all its creatures.

In Genesis 3, Adam and Eve rebelled against God's command at the prompting of the serpent. In doing so, they forfeited the dominion mandate to the Kingdom of Darkness, which assumed authority over the earth (Eph. 2:2, 2 Cor. 4:4.). The result is that all of mankind has been enslaved to this kingdom and feels the effects of this bondage.

St. Augustine, a fourth-century theologian, writes of two conflicting cities: the City of God, often referred to in scripture as the New Jerusalem, and the City of Man, or the world. He rightly describes these two cities as having separate origins and destinations, though they are both intermixed in our current time. Jesus speaks of this temporary intermingling in Matthew 13, referring to the people of God as wheat and the sons of perdition as tares, a semi-toxic plant closely resembling wheat. The two grew up together in the same field, initially inseparable and indistinguishable, though at the time of harvest, the tares are gathered and burned while the wheat is harvested. Jesus explains this is a type of judgment on the final day.

The two cities, as we will call them, originated on Earth in Genesis 3. Adam and all his posterity were surrendered to the rulership of Satan and his kingdom. Leading up to the great flood, the wickedness of mankind increased at an exponential rate as each generation outdid the last in their levels of depravity. By the tenth generation from Adam, the sin of the earth was so great that God had no choice left but to holocaust all life in order to preserve the righteous lineage of the Messiah through the offspring of Noah.

After the flood, humanity quickly backslid again. By the time of Abraham, it seemed that the entirety of mankind was worshipping one pantheon of gods or another, so-called gods that were really Satan and his angels. As Satan built up his kingdom and once again went to work building up generational strongholds of iniquity, God was quietly at work in the bloodline of David to bring about the Messiah, the one who was pointed to throughout the Old Testament; this Messiah was the promised deliverer for the City of God, still cruelly occupied by the enemy.

God painted an intricate picture of this messianic promise through the entirety of his word in the Old Testament, showing how his Messiah would be primarily a deliverer from bondage. Every action of Israel reflected this spiritual reality of bondage and liberation. The Israelites were enslaved by Egypt, and God delivered them. The Canaanites oppressed them, and the Lord raised up judges. Then the Assyrians invaded, and God saved Jerusalem. Later, he would deliver his people from exile in Babylon. All this time, the prophets pointed out that the real bondage was never physical but spiritual. Physical liberation never brought lasting relief. But the Lord promised a time when he would vanquish his people's iniquity, change their hearts, and give them a new nature (Ezek. 36:26, Mic. 7:19).

Up until the time of Christ, attempts at expelling demons were limited to these "magical" exorcisms, both in Jewish and pagan circles. These lengthy ceremonies involved spices, incense, and various religious articles. Pagan exorcists would invoke various deities and use drugs, potions, or charms, while Jews would invoke names of God and multiple angels or archangels. For Jews, at least, the appropriate word at the right time was essential to the exorcism.[1] These attempts of humanity to throw off the shackles of Satan were marked by a position of weakness. Demons need to be placated, warded off, or appeased. At best, Jews may have been able to invoke the Lord's help. But at the end of the day, humanity was in bondage.

The great hope of humanity was that one day, the Messiah would come and crush the serpent's head; bring deliverance from bondage to sin, sickness, and the Kingdom of Darkness; and restore creation to the way it was intended to be.

1 Patrick Toner, "Exorcist," in *The Catholic Encyclopedia*, vol. 5. (New York: Robert Appleton Company, 1909), accessed July 12, 2021, http://www.newadvent.org/cathen/05711a.htm.

# CHAPTER 2

# THE MINISTRY OF JESUS AND THE APOSTLES:
## THE LIBERATION OF MANKIND
### AD 30-80

And he came to Nazareth, where He had been brought up; and as was his custom, He entered the synagogue on the Sabbath, and stood up to read. And the book of the prophet Isaiah was handed to him. And he opened the book, and found the place where it was written, "The Spirit of the Lord is upon me, because He has anointed me to preach the gospel to the poor, He has sent me to proclaim release to the captives, and recovery of sight to the blind, to set free those who are oppressed and to proclaim the favorable year of the Lord." (Luke 4:16-19)

As the Lord introduced his public ministry that day in Nazareth, he reminded the people of the hope of the Messiah: freedom. Each facet of this proclamation connects to liberation from the satanically governed fallen world. Bringing good news to the poor, which we know in hindsight would be the saving message of grace, freedom to captives and prisoners, not of Rome, but sin, recovery of sight to both the spiritually and physically blind, and finally, the year of God's favor, reminiscence of a reversal of the curse. The earthly ministry of the Lord was a ministry of freedom. As he said in John 8:34–36, sin is a slave master, and he came to set the captives free.

For this historical study of spiritual warfare and exorcism, we will examine the major exorcisms of Jesus and the apostles as recorded in Acts. This chapter is not intended to be a theological exposition of all the New Testament says about spiritual warfare. Other resources have done that well already.[2]

## The Seven Major Exorcisms of Christ

Christ's ministry was marked by preaching, exorcism, and healing. These three central ministries, along with teaching and training his disciples, represent his early ministry's thrust. We know that Christ expelled demons on numerous occasions and that it was often associated with healing (Matt. 8:16, Luke 13:31–32, etc.). However, the gospel writers give us seven more detailed pictures of Christ's ministry of exorcism, which we will examine more closely.

### The Man in the Synagogue

³¹Then He went down to Capernaum, a city of Galilee, and was teaching them on the Sabbaths. ³²And they were astonished at His teaching, for His word was with

---

2    Ed Murphy's *The Handbook for Spiritual Warfare* is an excellent systematic theology on spiritual warfare.

authority. [33]Now in the synagogue there was a man who had a spirit of an unclean demon. And he cried out with a loud voice, [34]saying, "Let *us* alone! What have we to do with You, Jesus of Nazareth? Did You come to destroy us? I know who You are—the Holy One of God!" [35]But Jesus rebuked him, saying, "Be quiet, and come out of him!" And when the demon had thrown him in *their* midst, it came out of him and did not hurt him. [36]Then they were all amazed and spoke among themselves, saying, "What a word this *is!* For with authority and power He commands the unclean spirits, and they come out." [37]And the report about Him went out into every place in the surrounding region. (Luke 4:31–37).

v. 33. The first observation of this text is the location: the man was in the synagogue. Some scholars have suggested that the man and the other Jews were aware of his demonism and didn't care or do anything about it, but these arguments are unconvincing. Murphy points out that synagogues were attended primarily by pious people who were there to worship God. Further, Capernaum was a mixed city, and Jews in such mixed cities formed tight communities. The man was most likely an observant Jew, unaware of his condition and typically in his right mind.[3] Lest it is thought that this was some anomaly, Mark tells us Jesus toured the synagogues throughout all of Galilee, teaching and exorcising demons regularly (1:39).

In Luke's account, he clarified that this was an unclean, evil spirit, as the word "demon" would have been neutral to his Greek

---

3    Ed Murphy, *The Handbook for Spiritual Warfare*, rev. ed. (Nashville, TN: Thomas Nelson, 1996), 270–271.

audience. At some point in Christ's teaching, the demon reacted violently, arrested control of the man, and verbally protested. According to Murphy, the "question" isn't really a question but a protestation of Christ's teaching, probably on the salvation teaching quoted at the beginning of the chapter.[4] The demon further protests that they have nothing and want nothing in common with Christ before rightfully acknowledging Christ's humanity (Jesus of Nazareth) and his divinity (Holy One of God).[5] There is a change in pronouns from "I" to "we" throughout the demonic vocalization, probably suggesting that the demon was speaking for a group.[6]

v. 35. Jesus's first response was to silence the demon. In a panicked attempt to defend itself, the demon attempted to breach the messianic secret, which would hinder Jesus's earthly ministry, aggravating Jews and threatening Roman authorities.[7] Next, Jesus commands the spirit to come out. A violent manifestation ensues. Mark adds that the spirit causes convulsions. This episode showed that Jesus's exorcism was not sterile but a battle. Wiersbe and Henry both call this a last, futile attempt to resist Christ's command, perhaps by attempting to injure the man on the way out.[8] If this is the case, it was unsuccessful, as Luke explains, "... without injuring him."

vv. 36–37. This scandalous scene at Church leads to the beginning of Christ's fame. Both Luke and Mark record this as the first *public* miracle, directly leading to his rise in influence. Apparently,

---

4   Murphy, 272.

5   Warren W. Wiersbe, *The Bible Exposition Commentary: New Testament*, vol 1, 2nd ed. (Colorado Springs, CO: David C. Cook, 2008), 113.

6   Murphy, *Handbook for Spiritual Warfare*, 273.

7   Wiersbe, *Bible Exposition Commentary: New Testament*, 113.

8   Wiersbe, 113.

this exorcism was so superior to that of the Jews that it spoke of Christ having authority (v. 36) and was considered a notable miracle.

## Summary

The following observations can be made from this exorcism: (1) Jesus exorcised observant Jews during synagogue meetings. The demonized man, and by extension those delivered throughout the region, i.e., Mark 1:39, were in their right minds, enough to the degree they could attend synagogue without causing a commotion. (2) The demon had a violent, physical, and vocal manifestation, which did not stop until it was completely dispossessed. (3) The demon made a truthful, though spiteful, confession. (4) Exorcism was a means of gaining both positive and negative attention in the ministry of Christ.

## The Demoniac of the Gadarenes

¹They came to the other side of the sea, into the country of the Gerasenes. ²When He got out of the boat, immediately a man from the tombs with an unclean spirit met Him, ³and he had his dwelling among the tombs. And no one was able to bind him anymore, even with a chain; ⁴because he had often been bound with shackles and chains, and the chains had been torn apart by him and the shackles broken in pieces, and no one was strong enough to subdue him. ⁵Constantly, night and day, he was screaming among the tombs and in the mountains, and gashing himself with stones. ⁶Seeing Jesus from a distance, he ran up and bowed down before Him; ⁷and shouting with a loud voice,

he said, "What business do we have with each other, Jesus, Son of the Most High God? I implore You by God, do not torment me!" **⁸**For He had been saying to him, "Come out of the man, you unclean spirit!" **⁹**And He was asking him, "What is your name?" And he said to Him, "My name is Legion; for we are many." **¹⁰**And he *began* to implore Him earnestly not to send them out of the country. **¹¹**Now there was a large herd of swine feeding nearby on the mountain. **¹²***The demons* implored Him, saying, "Send us into the swine so that we may enter them." **¹³**Jesus gave them permission. And coming out, the unclean spirits entered the swine; and the herd rushed down the steep bank into the sea, about two thousand *of them*; and they were drowned in the sea. **¹⁴**Their herdsmen ran away and reported it in the city and in the country. And *the people* came to see what it was that had happened. **¹⁵**They came to Jesus and observed the man who had been demon-possessed sitting down, clothed and in his right mind, the very man who had had the "legion"; and they became frightened. **¹⁶**Those who had seen it described to them how it had happened to the demon-possessed man, and *all* about the swine. **¹⁷**And they began to implore Him to leave their region. (Mark 5:1–17)

vv. 1–2 In contrast to the subtle, hidden demons in the man at the synagogue, here is an extremely severe case of demonization; this man was driven to insanity by these spirits, living among the tombs. These were caves cut out of the limestone hills on the lakeside.

vv. 3–5 Not only did this case of demonism cause insanity, but it produced supernatural strength in the victim. He was a menace to the surrounding people, who tried to subdue and bind him, though they were unsuccessful. Murphy points out that most commentators will use these severe symptoms of demonization as a rule for what any demonic activity would look like.[9] Not only is this contrary to the experience of those in deliverance ministry, such as Dr. Murphy, but it is not congruent with the accounts of exorcism in the scriptures. This case was clearly the most severe of those recorded, standing above others in the Gospels and Acts in outlandish, supernatural symptoms.

v. 6 When the man sees Jesus, he runs toward him rather than away as we might expect. It is unlikely that the demons prompted the man to run toward Christ; when demons manifest in contemporary settings, they will more often run away from the authority of Christ.[10] More likely, the man himself, in a moment of clarity, somehow recognized Christ and ran toward him. On this note, Murphy makes a case that the man was ethnically Jewish, seeing as how he acted in line with the Jewish understanding of demon possession, rather than another cultural disposition.[11] Further, if he were not ethnically Jewish, it would represent a break in the practice of Christ, healing and delivering almost exclusively Jews. It may also be noted that Matthew's account records two demoniacs confront-

---

9   Murphy, *Handbook for Spiritual Warfare*, 279.
10  I have seen on several occasions violent demonic manifestations where the victim ran away, in an unconscious state, from the source of authority. Others with prolonged experience in deliverance ministry have witnessed such episodes as well.
11  Murphy, 279. The theory Murphy puts forward, on the citation of other scholars, is that demons work within the cultural and psychological framework of their victim. In other words, demons act how their victim expects them to act.

ing Christ (8:28) and does not give as many details toward the res-
olution. Some have postulated that the other demoniac *ran away*,
hence why Mark and Luke only record the one who was delivered.[12]

vv. 7–8 The demons react with the same defiance as the man in
the synagogue, asking the rhetorical question about what they have
in common. Further, they "implore" Christ to let them alone. This
word can also be translated as "adjure," a word used by Jewish exorcists to expel demons. The demonic host, in extreme defiance, was
trying to deliver themselves from Christ's presence! This defiance is
further seen in v. 8, as Jesus "had been" commanding the spirits to
come out. That means the spirits did not immediately obey Jesus,
and we don't know how long they resisted their defeat before they
were finally expelled.

v. 9 After Christ's typical method did not work, he asked the
spirit his name. Some have suggested that this was simply for the
benefit of the spectators to see what a great miracle it was,[13] though
this is unconvincing, seeing as how their defeat was delayed.
Murphy suggests that it was to gain insight into the man's situation,[14] and this is possible. As we will see in the following pages,
those battling demons have repeated this tactic throughout history.
Somehow, it works well enough for Christ to use it. The scripture
doesn't tell us how exactly it works, and we must accept that we see
through a glass darkly (1 Cor. 13:12).

vv. 10–12 The demons request that Jesus does not send them
out of the region. Perhaps their ability or influence would have been

---

12  John Goguen, Th.M., in conversation with the author.
13  Matthew Henry, *Matthew Henry's Commentary on the Whole Bible: Complete and
    Unabridged*, vol. 5 (Peabody, MA: Hendrickson Publishers, 1991), 387.
14  Murphy, *Handbook for Spiritual Warfare*, 282.

limited due to a connection with the regional principalities and powers. Further, we see that they prefer some sort of flesh, in this case, pigs, over being expelled into the "dry places" (Luke 11:24).

v. 13 After the spirits go into the pigs, the herd is driven insane and goes into the water. It's often questioned why Jesus allowed this. If the herders were Jewish, then it's clear that they were violating the law anyway. If not, it may be that the demise of the herd proved the deliverance on a wider scale than would have otherwise been possible.[15]

vv. 14–17 The response of the crowds is telling. Rather than rejoicing at such a miracle, they are terrified and "implore" Jesus to leave the region, echoing the same request of the demons that were just defeated.

In this account, we see Jesus delivering the most severely demonized person in scripture. We observe that (1) unlike other accounts of Jesus's exorcism, this one was not settled in a matter of seconds with one command. These spirits resisted for an undetermined period of time. (2) Despite the severe degree of demonism, the man still ran toward Jesus, and Christ didn't exorcise someone who didn't want freedom.[16] (3) The Lord used a simple form of what we will later call combative dialogue. (4) In this case, the demonization was so severe it appears the demons were in a constant state of manifestation, unlike the other accounts in the Gospels.

## The Syrophoenician Woman

[21] Jesus went away from there and withdrew into the district of Tyre and Sidon. [22] And a Canaanite woman from

---

15  Murphy, 282.

16  The man's desire for freedom is further clarified by his response in vv. 18–20.

that region came out and *began* to cry out, saying, "Have mercy on me, Lord, Son of David; my daughter is cruelly demon-possessed." [23] But He did not answer her a word. And His disciples came and implored Him, saying, "Send her away, because she keeps shouting at us." [24] But He answered and said, "I was sent only to the lost sheep of the house of Israel." [25] But she came and *began* to bow down before Him, saying, "Lord, help me!" [26] And He answered and said, "It is not good to take the children's bread and throw it to the dogs." [27] But she said, "Yes, Lord; but even the dogs feed on the crumbs which fall from their masters' table." [28] Then Jesus said to her, "O woman, your faith is great; it shall be done for you as you wish." And her daughter was healed at once. (Matt. 15:21–28)

vv. 21–22. The Lord comes to the district around Tyre and Sidon, his only recorded ministry outside of Israelite territory. A woman called a "Canaanite" here is the only reference to such an ethnicity within the New Testament. The point is that she was *not* an Israelite and was outside of the Abrahamic covenant, which is central to the account. Despite her Gentile, pagan background, she acknowledges him as the Messiah, calling him the "Son of David." Henry points out that the woman's description of her daughter's condition is "cruelly" possessed, as an especially severe degree of demonization.[17]

v. 23. The Lord initially ignored the woman's cry. The disciples began to ask the Lord to dismiss her, as she was apparently insistent

---

17   Henry, *Commentary on the Whole Bible*, 176.

to the point of their irritation. The response makes sense when we understand the Lord previously forbade the disciples to minister to Gentiles, so he would ignore them himself while they attempted to send her away. The reluctance shows the rule of faith by which Christ healed and delivered: "Your faith has made you well" (Matt. 9:22, Mark 10:52, Luke 18:42, etc.).

v. 24. After the woman had insisted for some time, the Lord qualifies his silence by exampling his mission to the wayward people of God. As mentioned, the Lord himself commanded his men only to heal, exorcise, and minister to those in Israel.

vv. 25–27 The woman avails herself of humility, faith, and submission to Christ. She now identifies herself with God's people as much as she can. The Lord further confirms that his ministry does not belong to the Gentiles or *unbelievers* but belongs to the "children" of God. It isn't right to take that ministry and give it to unbelievers. The woman's response represents a further condition of faith and humility; she begs for whatever little bit of help the Lord is willing to offer her.

v. 28 Christ acknowledges the legitimacy of her faith and delivers her daughter. Wiersbe explains that Christ was using this line of questioning to flush out and build up the woman's faith.[18] This is true, though I would add that the Lord knew this woman's faith was adamant from the beginning. What he did was more for the benefit of the disciples and readers of the Gospels to see the rule of faith; the Lord did not exorcise unbelievers; he calls deliverance the children's bread and the right due to God's people. The short delay in deliverance was not truly due to this woman's ethnicity but to

---

18  Wiersbe, *Bible Exposition Commentary: New Testament*, 54.

show the disciples that faith was necessary for coming to Christ for salvation or any other benefit. However, this concept would not be fully understood until later in Acts. Further, this deliverance did not require the laying on of hands or even a verbal command from Christ. He willed her free from a distance, and she was free instantly.

This case shows that the Lord was interested in ministering to a particular group of people, namely those who had faith in him. The Gentiles were initially excluded, not because of their ethnicity, but their religion. As we see later in Acts, the Gentiles come to Christ in droves; those who put their faith in him are the principal recipients of supernatural ministry.

## Exorcism of the Mute

³²As they went out, behold, they brought to Him a man, mute and demon-possessed. ³³And when the demon was cast out, the mute spoke. And the multitudes marveled, saying, "It was never seen like this in Israel!" ³⁴But the Pharisees said, "He casts out demons by the ruler of the demons." (Matt. 9:32–34, NKJV)

v. 32 Shortly after healing two blind men in the proceeding verses, the crowd brings forward a mute man, whose muteness was caused by a demon. Wiersbe points out that the scripture delineates between demonic problems and illness, but at times, demons cause physical ailments, as seen here.[19]

v. 33 This particular miracle caused a great excitement among the lay people. Though this was perhaps not as dramatic as other

---

19  Wiersbe, *Bible Exposition Commentary: New Testament*, 36.

exorcisms or healing miracles, it was especially public, unlike many of the private miracles. Despite the pangs of the crowd, and previous attempts to maintain the messianic secret, there was no attempt to conceal this miracle or take the man aside to deliver him.

v. 34 The religious leaders, by contrast, accused Jesus of black magic and bringing about the miracle by the Devil's power. This claim would return again in Jesus's ministry and in Jewish propaganda.

This relatively short account shows us that (1) demons can cause physical ailments and need to be cast out to bring about that cure. (2) Jesus performed exorcisms publicly, and they proved to be a major source of his popularity. Though he never "brought aside" a person he was exorcising, this was an especially public miracle. (3) Jesus's exorcism caused persecution from religious authorities.

## Exorcism of the Mute and Blind

[14]Jesus was driving out a demon that was mute. When the demon left, the man who had been mute spoke, and the crowd was amazed. [15]But some of them said, "By Beelzebul, the prince of demons, he is driving out demons." [16]Others tested him by asking for a sign from heaven. [17]Jesus knew their thoughts and said to them: "Any kingdom divided against itself will be ruined, and a house divided against itself will fall. [18]If Satan is divided against himself, how can his kingdom stand? I say this because you claim that I drive out demons by Beelzebul. [19]Now if I drive out demons by Beelzebul, by whom do your followers drive them out? So then, they will be your judges. [20]But if I drive out demons by the finger of God, then the kingdom of God has come upon

you. **21**"When a strong man, fully armed, guards his own house, his possessions are safe. **22**But when someone stronger attacks and overpowers him, he takes away the armor in which the man trusted and divides up his plunder. **23**"Whoever is not with me is against me, and whoever does not gather with me scatters. **24**"When an impure spirit comes out of a person, it goes through arid places seeking rest and does not find it. Then it says, 'I will return to the house I left.' **25**When it arrives, it finds the house swept clean and put in order. **26**Then it goes and takes seven other spirits more wicked than itself, and they go in and live there. And the final condition of that person is worse than the first." (Luke 11:14–26, NIV)

v. 14 Again, we have another deliverance from the demonic that results in healing. It is similar to the abovementioned account, where a mute was healed through exorcism. However, Matthew tells us that this man was both blind and mute (12:22). As soon as the demon left, the man was healed from his muteness (and blindness, though Luke does not recount that) without any additional action on the part of Christ. Like elsewhere, this miracle sparked incredible amazement.

v. 15 The Pharisees were not impressed. They attributed his miraculous power over demons to him secretly colluding with them. This accusation certainly got its mileage; later, critics of Christianity fabled that Christ had learned black magic while he spent a portion of his childhood in Egypt. Through such sorcery, he could cast out demons, heal the sick, and do other wonders. Even today, some occultists maintain that Jesus was, in fact, a master black magician who can even be learned from.[20] The name Beelzebub was a satirical demotion of the Canaanite god, Baal, who was considered a chief demon by the Jews of that time.[21] Beyond the exegetical particulars, the reaction of the religious establishment toward the ministry of deliverance was adverse, so much so that they called it a satanic counterfeit.

v. 16 Others, rather than go straight to blasphemy, challenged Christ to give a sign in the heavens as more sure proof that he was from God. Henry points out their logic: a pact with Satan may provide some power on Earth, but to summon some great thunder cloud, like Samuel or Moses, would prove His divine commissioning.[22] Even a clean-cut, quick exorcism that resulted in miraculous healing was no proof of anything. Deliverance ministry was not the package the Jews had ordered, and they wanted a "cleaner" miracle, somewhere preferably in the sky, that provided awe but no help for the sons of Adam.

vv. 17–18 Jesus refuses their request outright. In the first, they tempt God, which is a sin (Deut. 6:16). Further, it is an insult after the Lord has done something so wonderful to have the miracle reviled, and a "better" one asked in its place. The Lord, however, does not point this out. He simply explains the illogic of their accusation. Satan cannot effectively bring deliverance to people from himself. Not only is it a detriment to his kingdom, but it is against his nature to do good. Sure enough, there are exorcisms through the use of magic, though they cannot do what Christ

---

20   The Temple of Witchcraft in Salem, NH, published a teaching called "Jesus of Nazareth" that painted Jesus as magician who ought to be emulated, when understood through an occult lens.

21   Wiersbe, *Bible Exposition Commentary: New Testament*, 215.

22   Henry, *Commentary on the Whole Bible*, 561.

here does: bring actual deliverance resulting in the healing of two major maladies. This exorcism was entirely objective in its result and could not be a counterfeit, and Satan would never truly shoot himself in the foot.

vv. 19–20 The Jews also exorcised demons by invoking God's names, burning incense, and reciting scriptures. If Jesus was casting out demons by magic, what power were these Jews using? Surely, black magic cannot outperform God in Israel? In reality, it was the Jews who used a system of ritual; though it may at times have been effective, by God's mercy, being the only possible source of help, it more closely resembled a magical incantation. The Lord ironically turns the table on his opponents. His exorcism was not only in God's name but by his "finger" or Spirit. Here, Jesus connects his exorcisms with the arrival of the Kingdom of God. As the Kingdom of God arrives, it cannot do so without upsetting, dislodging, and pushing back the Kingdom of Darkness.

vv. 21–22 Jesus likens Satan to a strongman that holds his possessions, fully armed. Henry points out the contrast that pagan exorcists did not disturb the goods, i.e., even if one demon fled, another would come and take its place, and the souls of men remained captive to Satan.[23] However, Christ is stronger than Satan and needs no other power to invoke besides himself. He himself overpowers Satan, disarms him, and plunders him of souls.

v. 23 At the point of resistance to Jesus's deliverance ministry, he points out that there is no neutrality; people either engage with him in this war of dispossession or are his opponents. He says this not of healing or preaching but only of exorcism. Not only are they

---

23  Henry, *Commentary on the Whole Bible*, 562.

not with him, but they "scatter" or, by their opposition or passivity, are hindering this campaign.

v. 24–26 The danger of passivity in this was shown by the Lord, who explains how demons may leave a man, their "house," and come back. Once a spirit left, if the house were vacant, it would come back and invite all his friends, making the last state worse than before. This is often the case in magical exorcism.[24]

The theological significance in this account is not in the exorcism itself, which comprises only one verse and contains no new theological insight. The significance is in the response of the Pharisees and how Jesus confronted them. The religious establishment was disturbed by Jesus's ministry and accused it of being satanic. Jesus confronts them with the ignorance of such an accusation and, in Matthew's account, accuses them of blaspheming the Holy Spirit, a sin that could never be forgiven.

## The Moonstruck Boy

[17]A man in the crowd answered, "Teacher, I brought you my son, who is possessed by a spirit that has robbed him of speech. [18]Whenever it seizes him, it throws him to the ground. He foams at the mouth, gnashes his teeth and becomes rigid. I asked your disciples to drive out the spirit, but they could not." [19]"You unbelieving generation," Jesus replied, "how long shall I stay with you? How long shall I put up with you? Bring the boy to me." [20]So they brought him. When the spirit saw Jesus, it

---

24 Observed by contemporaries in deliverance ministry. Magical, pagan, or otherwise satanically induced exorcism often results in the temporary cure of the condition, only later to be replaced by something worse.

immediately threw the boy into a convulsion. He fell to the ground and rolled around, foaming at the mouth. ²¹Jesus asked the boy's father, "How long has he been like this?" "From childhood," he answered. ²²"It has often thrown him into fire or water to kill him. But if you can do anything, take pity on us and help us." ²³"'If you can'?" said Jesus. "Everything is possible for one who believes." ²⁴Immediately the boy's father exclaimed, "I do believe; help me overcome my unbelief!" ²⁵When Jesus saw that a crowd was running to the scene, he rebuked the impure spirit. "You deaf and mute spirit," he said, "I command you, come out of him and never enter him again." ²⁶The spirit shrieked, convulsed him violently, and came out. The boy looked so much like a corpse that many said, "He's dead." ²⁷But Jesus took him by the hand and lifted him to his feet, and he stood up. ²⁸After Jesus had gone indoors, his disciples asked him privately, "Why couldn't we drive it out?" ²⁹He replied, "This kind can come out only by prayer." (Mark 9:17–29, NIV)

vv. 17–18 This account takes place immediately after the transfiguration. Jesus comes down the mount with Peter, James, and John and finds the rest of his disciples arguing with a group of Pharisees. I surmise it had to do with the previous failure of the men to drive out the demon, as we later find out. Jesus inquires about the argument, but before receiving a reply, the father of the boy calls out to him and explains what is wrong with the child; a demon caused the child to be mute, a case we have seen before. However, this spirit also periodically seized the child, causing a condition similar to epilepsy. The nine apostles present were unable to expel the demon from the child.

v. 19 The Lord responds with frustration over the condition of that generation. Henry cites two opinions: it is either a rebuke to the disciples for their inability to exercise the power he gave them or a rebuke to the scribes who rejoiced over the defunct deliverance. In Matthew's account, he also calls them a "perverse" generation. It may be that "faithless" is a rebuke to the disciples and "perverse" a rebuke to the scribes.[25]

v. 20 As soon as the boy comes close to Christ, the spirit goes into a demonic manifestation. Contemporary deliverance ministries often observe that spirits will go into manifestation when they are threatened for whatever reason. The described epileptic condition manifests itself as well.

v. 21–22 While the demon is manifesting, Jesus does not immediately expel the spirit, nor does he command the manifestation to cease. He asks the father when this condition began. It began very early in the child's life, and now the father adds that it often tries to kill him by throwing him into water or fire. His emotions probably escalate as he remembers the horror and watches the manifestation before him, and he bursts into a desperate plea for help.

vv. 23–24 Jesus is taken aback by the doubtful statement as to whether or not the Son of God would be able to deliver the boy and explains all things are possible with faith. The father cries back, asking for help in his faith. Faith, here, is the central question of the passage, showing that it is the necessary ingredient for the supernatural.

---

25  Henry, *Commentary on the Whole Bible*, 413.

vv. 25–27 *When Jesus saw a crowd was gathering rapidly* and thus threatening to expose the messianic secret, he finally commanded the spirit *by name or function* to leave the boy and forbid it to enter him again. Once Jesus rebuked the spirit, the convulsions *increased* as the spirit departed until finally, the boy collapsed. The violence of the manifestation and collapse of the boy was what probably gave occasion for the audience to assume he was dead. The Lord took the boy and raised him up, proving his life and freedom.

vv. 28–29 The disciples later question him about why they could not cast out the demon. The Lord explains that *this kind* only comes out through prayer and fasting. In Matthew's version, he says that their unbelief was the reason for the failure. Some have connected *this kind* with the unbelief that the Lord speaks of in Matthew, denoting that their unbelief will not depart without prayer or fasting. A more honest reading will connect *this kind* with kinds of demons, of which this spirit was particularly powerful. Henry explains, "The disciples must not think to do their work always with a like ease; some services call them to take more than ordinary pains; but Christ can do that with a word's speaking, which they must prevail for the doing of by *prayer and fasting.*"[26]

In this passage, we see again a confrontation between the spiritual warfare of Christ and his followers and the religionists. Faith appears as the central fuel for exorcism's success or lack thereof. Further, in this case, the symptoms of demonism were not always present but only came in severe episodes. We also learn that there are degrees of demonic power and, likewise, various degrees of effort that must be exerted to deal with it.

---

26  Henry, *Commentary on the Whole Bible*, 413.

## Woman with the Spirit of Infirmity

<sup>10</sup>And He was teaching in one of the synagogues on the Sabbath. <sup>11</sup>And there was a woman who for eighteen years had had a sickness caused by a spirit; and she was bent double, and could not straighten up at all. <sup>12</sup>When Jesus saw her, He called her over and said to her, "Woman, you are freed from your sickness." <sup>13</sup>And He laid His hands on her; and immediately she was made erect again and *began* glorifying God. <sup>14</sup>But the synagogue official, indignant because Jesus had healed on the Sabbath, *began* saying to the crowd in response, "There are six days in which work should be done; so come during them and get healed, and not on the Sabbath day." <sup>15</sup>But the Lord answered him and said, "You hypocrites, does not each of you on the Sabbath untie his ox or his donkey from the stall and lead him away to water *him*? <sup>16</sup>And this woman, a daughter of Abraham as she is, whom Satan has bound for eighteen long years, should she not have been released from this bond on the Sabbath day?" <sup>17</sup>As He said this, all His opponents were being humiliated; and the entire crowd was rejoicing over all the glorious things being done by Him. (Luke 13:10–17)

vv.10–11 As in the first account we examined, the Lord Jesus is again teaching in the synagogue, though he is not alone. A woman there had a severe deformity that prevented her from standing up straight for eighteen years. Though it was probably unknown to the other congregants, Christ saw that hers was not a natural ailment, but a

deformity caused by a *spirit of infirmity*. This is the third of seven accounts where demonization is expressed only through an infirmity.

vv. 12–13 The Lord calls the woman and brings her ailment into the public. Wiersbe points out that Jesus "exposes" her disease in front of everyone when we cross this with Matthew 12:13 and that this was to "expose" Satan.[27] This was not a private healing. Jesus did not take the woman into the back room to deliver her, nor did he see it as an interruption of the meeting. The Lord exercised and healed the woman by first verbally saying that she was "loosed," or untied, unbound from her infirmity. He then laid his hands on her, and she straightened up. It is possible the "loosing" expelled the demon and the laying on of hands enacted the healing. Her response, naturally, was glorifying God.

v. 14 The synagogue administrator was not thrilled about the healing. Much like several previous accounts, deliverance for the captives seems to have been a big point of contention with the enemies of Christ. He didn't have the audacity to rebuke Christ, who was teaching after all, so he rebuked the congregation. His rebuke is obnoxious, saying that the people ought to come on other days to be healed. Who would heal them? He didn't think his statement through or was perhaps comparing Christ in the same category as "quacks and mountebanks."[28]

v.15 Unlike the synagogue official who beat around the bush, Christ rebuked him directly, pointing out that everyone was willing to "loose" their animals to be fed and watered on the Sabbath. It's commonly understood that it was *cruel* to do otherwise. Is not

---

27  Wiersbe, *Bible Exposition Commentary: New Testament*, 225.

28  Henry, *Commentary on the Whole Bible*, 584.

the loosing of an animal to water it, however mundane and easy it is, more work than speaking a word and touching with a hand?

v. 16 Now if we can untie the ox and the ass, why not loose this *daughter of Abraham*? Wiersbe rightly points out that this refers to the woman's spiritual condition, not her physical ethnicity. That means she was a converted person who was bound by a demon, an uncomfortable reality Wiersbe is hesitant to admit.[29] Henry, on the other hand, sees no problem with the fact. Rather, he loosely connects this passage with the Syrophoenician woman, pointing out that as a believer, she is the very person "entitled" to deliverance.[30]

v. 17 Christ's clear rebuke was a humiliation to his opponents and pointed out the rightness of what was done for the woman. The rest of the crowd accepted the miracle and its logic and praised God.

This passage is so abundantly clear that a believer was bound by a demon it is almost impossible for commentators to wiggle out of its implications without resorting to theological gymnastics. But the reality is that this exorcism was not the exception; it was the rule. Derek Prince writes that the people the Lord delivered from the demonic were "observant Jews who met every Sabbath in the synagogue and spent the rest of the week caring for their families, tending their fields, fishing the sea and minding their shops."[31] In all seven of these passages, there is no clear example of a person being delivered who did not express some faith in God, somehow or another. Several cried or ran to Christ. Several were found worshipping God in the synagogue. In one case, the Lord withheld

---

29    Wiersbe, *Bible Exposition Commentary: New Testament*, 225
30    Henry, *Commentary on the Whole Bible*, 585.
31    Derek Prince, *They Shall Expel Demons: What you Need to Know about Demons—Your Invisible Enemy* (Grand Rapids, MI: Chosen Books, 1998), 21.

deliverance until faith was proved; in another, the Lord calls the woman healed a legitimate believer.

## Exorcism in the Ministry of Jesus

Exorcism was not new when Jesus began to cast out demons. However, the way in which he did it was revolutionary. Previous exorcisms were performed from a place of weakness, seeking to invoke some stronger spiritual force to subdue a possessing demon. However, Jesus was himself a stronger spiritual force and delegated that strength to his followers. The exorcisms of Jesus were the most dramatic confrontation with the Kingdom of Darkness in his ministry and most directly connected with the arrival of the Kingdom of God.[32]

*Table I*

*The Exorcisms of Jesus*

| The Account | Reference | The Victim | The Malady | The Cure |
|---|---|---|---|---|
| The Man in the Synagogue | Mark 1:21–28, Luke 4:31–37 | A man in a synagogue at Capernaum. Most likely a regular worshipper who was unaware that he was demonized. | The scripture gives no indication. We can surmise that it was a subtle oppression. | The demon manifests and verbally engages Christ. The Lord forbids the spirit to speak further and commands it to come out verbally. The spirit convulses the man and then leaves. |

32 Graham H. Twelftree, *In the Name of Jesus: Exorcism among Early Christians* (Grand Rapids, MI: Baker Academic, 2007), 128.

| | | | | |
|---|---|---|---|---|
| The Demoniac of the Gadarenes | Matt. 8:28–34,<br><br>Mark 5:1–20,<br><br>Luke 8:26–39 | The man was probably a Jew living in the Decapolis. We do not know the background of his faith, but on seeing Christ, he ran to him. | The man was driven to insanity, living in a near-constant state of demonic manifestation. He cut himself, lived in the tombs, and howled like an animal. He also displayed supernatural strength. | The Lord verbally commands the spirit several times without it coming out. He interrogates it, finds its name, and then allows it to go out into a herd of pigs. |
| The Syrophoenician Woman | Matt. 15:21–28,<br><br>Mark 7:24–30 | The woman in the account intercedes for her daughter, who is demonized. Both are Gentiles, who most likely were pagans. However, the woman displayed legitimate faith. | The demon seemed to have caused some sort of physical suffering, though the woman knew that the suffering was demonic and unnatural. | The Lord granted the woman's request and proclaimed that the daughter was healed, without seeing her, without even commanding any spirits. |
| The Exorcism of the Mute | Matt 9:32–34 | Most likely a Jew. | The spirit caused muteness. | The passage gives very little detail, but it was most likely a verbal command. |

| The Exorcism of the Blind and Mute | Matt 12:22–32, Mark 3:20–30, Luke 11:14–23 | Most likely a Jew. | The spirit caused both blindness and mute-ness. | The passage gives very little detail, but it was most likely a verbal command. |
|---|---|---|---|---|
| The Moonstruck Boy | Matt. 17:14–20, Luke 9:37–43 | A young Jewish boy, whose father sup-plicated on his behalf for his healing. | The spirit caused severe epilepsy and suicidal tendencies. | The Lord inter-views the father and then com-mands the spirit to come out. He indicates to the apostles that prayer and fasting would have been effective here. |
| The Woman with the Spirit of Infirmity | Luke 13:10–17 | A devout, older woman whom Jesus classified as a daughter of Abra-ham. | The spirit bent the woman's back super-naturally, so she could not stand up. | The Lord commanded the spirit to go and laid hands on the woman. |

## Spiritual Warfare in Acts

In the "Great Commission" of Matthew 28, the Lord commands the apostles, "Go therefore and make disciples of all nations, bap-tizing them in the name of the Father, the Son, and the Holy Spirit teaching them to observe *all* that I commanded you" (vv. 19–20a, emphasis mine). The Lord commanded and taught the apostles to preach, heal the sick, and cast out demons (Matt. 10:1, 8).

In Acts, we see primarily the story of the growth and develop-ment of the early Church. However, Luke prefaces his account by explaining that it is what Jesus *continued* to do and teach through the apostles (1:1–2). Therefore, it is not surprising that much of the activity of Christ's ministry is reflected throughout Acts, including confrontational spiritual warfare. There are three passages in which spiritual warfare is especially highlighted.

## Mass Deliverance in Samaria

⁴Therefore, those who had been scattered went about preaching the word. ⁵Philip went down to the city of Samaria and *began* proclaiming Christ to them. ⁶The crowds with one accord were giving attention to what was said by Philip, as they heard and saw the signs which he was performing. ⁷For *in the case* of many who had unclean spirits, they were coming out *of them* shouting with a loud voice; and many who had been paralyzed and lame were healed. ⁸So there was much rejoicing in that city. ⁹Now there was a man named Simon, who formerly was practicing magic in the city and astonishing the people of Samaria, claiming to be someone great; ¹⁰and they all, from smallest to greatest, were giving attention to him, saying, "This man is what is called the Great Power of God." ¹¹And they were giving him attention because he had for a long time astonished them with his magic arts. ¹²But when they believed Philip preaching the good news about the kingdom of God and the name of Jesus Christ, they were being baptized, men and women alike. ¹³Even Simon himself believed; and after being baptized, he continued on with Philip, and as he observed signs and great miracles taking place, he was constantly amazed. ¹⁴Now

when the apostles in Jerusalem heard that Samaria had received the word of God, they sent them Peter and John, [15]who came down and prayed for them that they might receive the Holy Spirit. [16]For He had not yet fallen upon any of them; they had simply been baptized in the name of the Lord Jesus. [17]Then they *began* laying their hands on them, and they were receiving the Holy Spirit. [18]Now when Simon saw that the Spirit was bestowed through the laying on of the apostles' hands, he offered them money, [19]saying, "Give this authority to me as well, so that everyone on whom I lay my hands may receive the Holy Spirit." [20]But Peter said to him, "May your silver perish with you, because you thought you could obtain the gift of God with money! [21]"You have no part or portion in this matter, for your heart is not right before God. [22]"Therefore repent of this wickedness of yours, and pray the Lord that, if possible, the intention of your heart may be forgiven you. [23]"For I see that you are in the gall of bitterness and in the bondage of iniquity." [24]But Simon answered and said, "Pray to the Lord for me yourselves, so that nothing of what you have said may come upon me." (Acts 8:4–24)

v. 4 The context of the previous passage is the persecution of the infant Church at Jerusalem, which began at the death of Stephen. Hellenistic Jews were the easiest targets, standing out from the native Hebraic Jews, hence why the apostles remained (v.1), and the Hellenistic Jews were scattered.[33]

---

33  Wiersbe, *Bible Exposition Commentary: New Testament*, 434.

v. 5 Philip broke a traditional barrier and went to a people who were theoretically further from God than the Jews, though not as far as Gentiles. Most commentators are most interested in this fact as far as the expansion of the gospel is concerned. This is not within the scope of our subject. What is important to note is that the Samaritans had the Torah and were also awaiting the Messiah, making Philip's preaching relevant.[34]

vv. 6–8 The first matter of spiritual warfare in this passage. The Samaritans pay very close attention to Philip's preaching. The reason they did was because they both *saw* and *heard* the miracles he was performing. The exorcism of *many* with unclean spirits is mentioned first, followed by people being healed from lameness and paralysis. Dr. Murphy connects the demonization with the physical ailments,[35] a reasonable theory given the frequent connection in the Gospels. Were those delivered converted before or after their deliverance? Commentators are divided on that matter, though there is general agreement that the miracles convinced the multitude of them to turn toward Christ. Finally, the result of all the miracles and conversion was great joy.

vv. 9–11 Simon Magus, as he was often called by later writers, was a magician who had previously captivated the people of the area. Marshall explains that the title "Great Power of God" was some sort of claim to divinity, be that either a heavenly being or some representation of God.[36] Murphy attributes the severe demo-

---

34    Ajith Fernando, *The NIV Application Commentary: Acts* (Grand Rapids, MI: Zondervan, 1998), 271.

35    Murphy, *Handbook for Spiritual Warfare*, 316.

36    I. Howard Marshall, *The Acts of the Apostles: An Introduction and Commentary* (Grand Rapids, MI: William B. Eerdmans Publishing Company, 1980), 165.

nization of the city to this rascally magician, who had so ensnared them with demonic power.[37]

vv. 12–13 Whatever magical powers Simon displayed, real or fictitious, paled greatly in comparison to the Gospel trident of evangelism, exorcism, and miracles, in the estimation of both the people and Simon himself. Luke tells us that Simon believed and was baptized. It is difficult for many commentators to accept that this means he was *born again*, especially in light of Peter's rebuke in vv. 22–24. Henry correctly states, "The Church and its ministers must go by a judgment of charity, as far as there is room for it," thus, Philip rightly baptized him.[38] It is difficult to imagine, having been a sorcerer one's whole life, that years of bad thinking would be erased in the baptistry on hearing and accepting the gospel. Conversion, especially *mass* conversion, is typically complete with an instant change in thinking. In Acts 19, some Christians had believed for some time and still practiced magic! woman in our Church was born again from the occult about two years before this writing. It took her three months to realize that much of her occult practice was displeasing to the Lord when she repented and abandoned it. We have here a similar situation. I agree with Dr. Murphy, who attributes most negative accounts of Simon to legend, and that we all have a trace of Simon Magus within us.[39]

vv. 14–18 Though these verses contain rich theological insight, they are beyond our subject. Suffice it to say that this author maintains that the Baptism of the Holy Spirit is an experience after conversion, as seems clear in this account. Fernando also points out

---

37  Murphy, *Handbook for Spiritual Warfare*, 316.
38  Henry, *Commentary on the Whole Bible*, 80.
39  Murphy, *Handbook for Spiritual Warfare*, 320.

that "there must have been some external manifestations, such as speaking in tongues, that gave unmistakable evidence," seeing as how Simon "saw" the spirit fell on the people.

vv. 19–24 Simon was especially drawn to this power, which seems to be painted as superior to the healing and delivering power of Philip. Peter very strongly rejects this offer. Marshall comments that Peter was consigning Simon and his money to damnation if he didn't repent.[40] This strong imprecation is comparable to Peter's rebuke in Acts 5, which resulted in two deaths. Simon's reply, and the fact that he did not die on the spot as Ananias and Sephira, may speak to the legitimacy of his conversion. Peter's description in v. 23 may be evidence that Simon was still demonized, though this is not certain.

This account shows evangelism, healing, and exorcism going hand in hand, in the same manner as the Gospels. Philip, being the only named evangelist of the New Testament, was involved in preaching, exorcising, and healing. In evangelism of unreached areas, there is often confrontation with occultists, which may either result in a confrontation, such as in Acts 13, or it may be a crude conversion.

### The Girl with Python

[16]It happened that as we were going to the place of prayer, a slave-girl having a spirit of divination met us, who was bringing her masters much profit by fortune-telling. [17]Following after Paul and us, she kept crying out, saying, "These men are bond-servants of

---

40   I. Howard Marshall, *The Acts of the Apostles: An Introduction and Commentary* (Grand Rapids, MI: William B. Eerdmans Publishing Company, 1980), 168.

the Most High God, who are proclaiming to you the way of salvation." ¹⁸She continued doing this for many days. But Paul was greatly annoyed, and turned and said to the spirit, "I command you in the name of Jesus Christ to come out of her!" And it came out at that very moment. ¹⁹But when her masters saw that their hope of profit was gone, they seized Paul and Silas and dragged them into the marketplace before the authorities, ²⁰and when they had brought them to the chief magistrates, they said, "These men are throwing our city into confusion, being Jews, ²¹and are proclaiming customs which it is not lawful for us to accept or to observe, being Romans." (Acts 16:16–21)

v. 16 Paul and the apostolic team made their ministry in Philippi by the river at the place of prayer. While doing so, there was a young girl who was demonized by a spirit of divination, or more accurately, Python, whom her owners were using for profit. The spirit of python was related in Greek culture to the oracles of Apollo at Delphi. Marshall explains that Python was also connected with ventriloquism.[41] This ability no doubt enhanced the girl's reputation.

v. 17 The girl was going about proclaiming that the apostles served the Most High God and proclaimed the way of salvation, a message that would not have been alien to a Greek audience.[42] At first glance, this is a strange confession coming from the Kingdom of Darkness. However, we may remember that demons had made

---

41   Marshall, 285
42   Marshall, 285.

truthful acknowledgments about Christ in the Gospels. In fact, in no exorcism in the Gospels or Acts did a spirit, while being confronted, speak a lie. In several Gospels' accounts, demonic acknowledgment of Christ may have been a maneuver to prematurely expose the messianic secret, though this explanation would not apply here. Henry makes two possible suggestions: (1) that the spirit was forced to acknowledge the gospel for God's glory, and (2) that it was attempting to legitimize its messages, either to the Church or the Gentiles, or both.[43] Of the two suggestions, I find the second more likely, since it is reflected more commonly throughout Church history,[44] though the first is not impossible.

v. 18 This happened many days before Paul took action, which puzzled commentators. Various theories have been surmised, such as Paul perhaps not realizing it was demonic at first or not caring. If our understanding of the exorcisms in the Gospels is correct, I suggest that Paul avoided exorcising the girl for the same reason Christ initially denied the Gentile woman her request. That is, she was not a believer, and deliverance from the demonic was the "children's bread." Whether that be the case or not, in the end, it was annoyance that motivated Paul; perhaps the girl's proclamations were muddying the waters between Christianity and paganism, or maybe she was gaining the interest of new believers, or perhaps Paul was personally annoyed. Whatever the case, he turned to cast out the spirit. NASB and most modern translations do a disservice to this verse, making it seem as though the spirit left instantly. The Greek reads that it came out within the hour. Henry

---

43   Henry, *Commentary on the Whole Bible*, 168.
44   Montanans being a notable example of demonic replication of charismatic gifts that sought to infiltrate the Church. See chapter 3.

rightly observes on this point that it took the apostle Paul time to expel this spirit, perhaps because it was strongly entrenched.[45] If our theory is correct, and most instances of deliverance in scripture were for or on behalf of believers, and this girl was not converted, then the elongated struggle further makes sense.

vv. 19–21 It should not come as a surprise that some people were very displeased with the deliverance ministry of Paul. The girl's owners took a profit loss. Not only did the girl most likely lose the ability to tell fortunes, but Apollo and his snakes were defeated in public by the name of Christ, discrediting their divinity. The owners rounded up a mob, pressed trumped-up charges, and ended up having Paul and Silas flogged and imprisoned, treatment illegal for Roman citizens.

This account shows exorcism continuing in public, accompanying the apostle's ministry. In typical fashion, Luke pits Christ's forces against the world's various occult powers, in this case, through a direct power encounter. Further, as was so often the case with Christ and would continue to be the case throughout the next twenty centuries, deliverance ministry was stiffly resisted. Paul had carried out evangelism, prayer, and teaching peaceably and only encountered persecution when he confronted the Devil.

## Christians and Magic in Ephesus

[11] God was performing extraordinary miracles by the hands of Paul, [12] so that handkerchiefs or aprons were even carried from his body to the sick, and the diseases left them and the evil spirits went out. [13] But also some

---

45    Henry, *Commentary on the Whole Bible*, 169.

of the Jewish exorcists, who went from place to place, attempted to name over those who had the evil spirits the name of the Lord Jesus, saying, "I adjure you by Jesus whom Paul preaches." [14] Seven sons of one Sceva, a Jewish chief priest, were doing this. [15] And the evil spirit answered and said to them, "I recognize Jesus, and I know about Paul, but who are you?" [16] And the man, in whom was the evil spirit, leaped on them and subdued all of them and overpowered them, so that they fled out of that house naked and wounded. [17] This became known to all, both Jews and Greeks, who lived in Ephesus; and fear fell upon them all and the name of the Lord Jesus was being magnified. [18] Many also of those who had believed kept coming, confessing and disclosing their practices. [19] And many of those who practiced magic brought their books together and *began* burning them in the sight of everyone; and they counted up the price of them and found it fifty thousand pieces of silver. [20] So the word of the Lord was growing mightily and prevailing. (Acts 19:11–20)

vv. 11–12 Ephesus was a center of occult magic during the first century, which is perhaps why Paul was empowered with "extraordinary miracles" beyond those seen in other apostolic missions. In this case, even objects associated with Paul could exorcise spirits and effect cures.

vv. 13–14 Paul's deliverance ministry had come to such notoriety that Jewish exorcists attempted to invoke the name of Jesus in the exorcisms. This reflects magical ritualism; the power of the spell rested not in the exorcist or spirit behind him but in the names invoked and the words used. Likewise, these men attempted to use the name of Christ as a magic spell, devoid of any relationship to him. "Sceva" was most likely not any real chief priest, but the title was adopted to give credibility to the family business.

vv. 15–16 During an exorcism, these Jewish magicians attempted to invoke the name of Christ. The spirit readily recognized the name of Jesus and Paul, who rightly used his name by challenging the magician's authority to use the name.[46] The demonized man quickly overpowered the seven, beating and stripping them.

v. 17 This story circulated the area widely and brought a strong sense of the fear of God.

vv. 18–19 The fear and reverence inspired not only unbelievers but put a repentant fire under the Church as well. What is astounding is that "those *who had* believed" (emphasis mine) began to confess magical practices. The pluperfect tense leaves no room for doubt that these were believers for some time before they had confessed their practices. Marshall comments, "Christians are not fully converted or perfected in an instant, and pagan ways of thinking can persist alongside genuine Christian experience."[47]

In this passage, we see the deliverance ministry of Paul as an expansionary element in the Ephesus mission. Further, the deeply ingrained occult thinking of legitimate Christians took time to dialogue fully. We also observe that demons continued to recognize Christ and his servants, as they did in the Gospels.

---

46  It is common in the experience of contemporary deliverance ministers, for demons to recognize and revile persons who are involved in deliverance.

47  Marshall, *Acts of the Apostles*, 330.

## Conclusions

Within the ten passages we examined, the following can be drawn. Exorcism was not limited to any particular context. The gospel writers saw fit to record diverse situations in which deliverance took place. Christ and the apostles used exorcism to cure physical ailments and mental disturbances and deliver those who may not have even known they were bound. These encounters occurred in conjunction with healing and preaching, in the synagogues, in the streets, and even in a cemetery. The war was fought on all fronts.

In the Gospels, Christ is the initial deliverer and shortly appoints the apostles especially to preach and drive out demons (Mark 3:14). This commission was later expanded beyond the twelve to include seventy other non-apostolic followers (Luke 10). Despite these specific appointments, the ministry of deliverance was not limited to Christ or those he appointed. Mark 16, if the reader accepts its validity as scripture,[48] qualifies any believer to drive out demons. Further, in Luke 9:49, a nominal follower of Christ is found casting out demons to the consternation of the apostles. However, Jesus endorses the action in his name. Exorcism appears to have been an all-inclusive ministry in the New Testament.

The people who were delivered in the Gospels and Acts were consistently those who either expressed some faith in Christ or were making some move toward him. It cannot be said that they were all "believers" in the strictest sense, in that there was no New Birth during the life of Christ. However, by Old Testament

---

48 Though the longer ending of Mark was probably not written by the original John Mark, it is still in the canon of scripture. We believe that the Holy Spirit preserved the scripture, and that protestant canon represents that preserved scripture, regardless of authorship.

standards, it seems that, generally, those who were delivered were those who were putting their faith in God. For those examples in Acts, there is not enough context to say they were believers or not, though there is a strong possibility that some were. Per the scripture, the doctrine of the demonization of demons is more strongly affirmed throughout the Bible beyond a simple examination of the exorcisms of Jesus. However, that topic is beyond the scope of this work, beyond examining it from a historical perspective.

Their general brevity and charismatic approach characterized the exorcisms of the New Testament. The power came from Christ himself, either through his person, as in the Gospels, or through believers, as in Acts. There was no power in rituals or objects. The closest possible examples are the items Paul used to expel demons in Acts 19, though this is only an incidental resemblance to ritual exorcism.

The significance of exorcism in the ministry of Christians would continue from the Gospels and play a significant role in the early Church. Those deliverances recorded above, and the great victory of Calvary, represent the beachhead to an extended campaign through the Devil out of the known world.

# CHAPTER 3

# PRE-NICENE ERA:

## THE APOSTOLIC TRIDENT AND THE THREE HUNDRED YEAR REVIVAL
### AD 80-312

## Miracles in the Early Church

Within a couple of centuries, Christianity supplanted traditional Greco-Roman paganism as the dominant religion; a religion that had centuries of cultural roots, governmental backing and funding, and support from every side. How did a suppressed religion spread so quickly? Historian Ramsay MacMullen asks the same question in his book *Christianizing the Roman Empire*. He concludes that typical modes of evangelism, such as public preaching, tracts, apologetic literature, etc., were all ineffective for one reason or another. What brought about conversions were miracles, or at least their reports.[49]

---

49 Ramsay MacMullen, *Christianizing the Roman Empire: A.D. 100–400* (New Haven, CT: Yale University Press, 1984), 25–41.

We know that Christians of the late second century believed that miracles were a leading cause of conversion,[50] and that from the late second century until the time of Augustine, Christian literature frequently referenced miracles of various kinds, including exorcism.

## The Problem of the Literature Gap

Though the records of Acts and the perspective of Christians from beyond the second century indicate that the Church was operating in miracles, very little literature from the early second century exists on exorcism or spiritual warfare. The writings from that time were often short, apologetic essays explaining and defending Christian belief. For some historians, this provides a problem for understanding the Evangelical Church. Were they experiencing the same power evangelism that was recorded in Acts? If they were, why weren't they writing about it? And if not, how do we explain the gap between what is described in Acts and the latter half of the second century?

A few suggestions have been proposed to understand this. Some believe that the lack of literature directly corresponds to a lack of experience, though I question this line of thinking. Some proponents of deliverance suggest that the lack of literature about spiritual warfare reflects that it was so common no writing was needed.[51] The truth is probably more moderate. Seeing the primitive and suppressed condition of the early second-century Church, it is not surprising that writing on spiritual warfare was sparse, as writing, *in general*, was sparse. When literature was necessary, the first need was to explain the new creed and to help differentiate Christianity from the Jewish tradition. Further, Christians hadn't

---

50   Justin Martyr, *II Apology.*
51   Larson suggests this solution in his International School of Exorcism.

yet developed much academia, and the ability to produce literature was also limited.

However, if we look at the historical context in Acts and what Church history records in the mid and late second century, we see plenty of miracle accounts, including plenty of exorcisms. It seems unlikely that exorcism and miracles were only a matter of interest in the first and late second centuries and that there was any sort of break in continuity between these generations. Exorcism during the early first century probably looked very similar to what is described in Acts and the late second century.

## The Late Second Century

### "Shepherd of Hermas"

One of the first documents that gives us a glimpse into the early Christian understanding of spiritual warfare is *Shepherd of Hermas* (AD 140)—a document "widely regarded in the early Church,"[52] which nearly became a part of the New Testament. The document describes spiritual warfare as the competition between demons and the Holy Spirit for intellectual, emotional, and spiritual real estate within the Christian. Areas of a person's mind, will, and emotion were either surrendered to God or subjected by Satan. *Hermas* further taught that if believers consistently surrendered more ground to the enemy, the Holy Spirit would eventually vacate, leaving the person to reprobation and death.[53]

*Hermas* does not teach anything about expelling demons through exorcism but recommends dispossession by a system of prayer, repen-

---

52  Twelftree, *In the Name of Jesus*, 212.
53  *Shepherd of Hermas* 34.7, 100.5.

tance, and surrender to the word of God to take back intellectual and emotional ground.[54] It's interesting to note that the first Church history document on spiritual warfare affirms the demonization of Christians and understands some sort of mental war between the Holy Spirit and the Devil through the process of sanctification within the Christian.

## Justin Martyr

Justin Martyr (AD 100–165) was one of the first notable Christian apologists and one of the most influential figures in the early Church, both on account of his skilled apologetics and his reported performance of miracles. Many will cite Justin as an example of early Church culture and an archetype of an early Church evangelist.

Unlike earlier Christian writers, Justin writes profusely on the Devil and spiritual warfare. He describes in detail the tactics of demons, entering into compacts and blood covenant agreements with men, thus enslaving them. They go on to use this influence to cause murders, wars, and general evil in the world. They attempt to destroy the Church using persecution from the outside and heresy from within. Heresy among Christians was one of the most pernicious problems caused by demons and one that could not be solved with just scriptural teaching; those under the influence of spirits of error needed deliverance before they could be properly instructed.[55] During his *Second Apology*, one of Justin's most significant works, his only evidence that Christ is superior to the gods of Rome is that Jesus's name has been effective to drive out demons the world over and in Rome itself, a fact apparently self-evident to his opponents.[56]

---

54  Twelftree, *In the Name of Jesus*, 213.
55  Justin Martyr, *2 Apol.* 5:4; *Dial.* 131:2; *1 Apol.* 26.
56  Justin Martyr, *2 Apology* 6:6.

For Justin, spiritual warfare is not an extracurricular activity or a job for specialists; deliverance from the demonic is the primary reason for Christ's coming (2 *Apol.* 6:5). He describes *many* Christians as exorcising demons (2 *Apol.* 6:6). There is no special office of exorcist, neither must one be an apostle or pastor to be employed in deliverance. Any lay Christian could cast out demons.

It is clear from Justin's literature and his contemporaries' writing that exorcism was not any sort of background or secondary ministry, but a primary thrust of the Church at this time. The worldview described by Justin is that of humanity in cruel subjection to sin and Satan. The only solution was the aggressive preaching of the gospel and the violent expulsion of demons. This spiritual war was not vague or invisible but played out through dramatic confrontations with demons and their subsequent humiliation. These public displays ever resounded in debate with pagans: how is it that this spirit, claiming to be the god you worship, quivers and shrieks at the name of Christ? This evidence alone was more than enough for Justin.

Justin's methodology of exorcism emphasized the power of the name of the Lord Jesus; the power of the name was not in its invocation but in the relationship of the exorcist to Christ.[57] Dr. Twelftree concludes, "Justin considered exorcism the most important weapon of evangelism Christians possessed against the various threats to the church in a demon-infested world."[58]

## Irenaeus of Lyon

Irenaeus of Lyon (AD 130–202) is considered to be the most influential theologian before Origen and one of the first to create what

---

57  Twelftree, *In the Name of Jesus*, 242.
58  Twelftree, 252.

we would call systematic theology. His primary work was defending orthodox Christianity against various heretical sects of his time, especially Gnosticism. Though he is most well known for his theological reasoning against erroneous theology, he also made a case for orthodox Christianity through miracles.

According to Irenaeus, miracles, including healing, revelatory gifts, and exorcism, were all present in the orthodox Church and were either absent or perverted in heretical groups; this was proof of their divine misalignment. Irenaeus points to the ineffectiveness of heretical exorcisms and their resemblance to pagan rituals. In contrast, Christian exorcism was based on "sympathy and compassion," while heretics charged money for their defunct exorcisms.[59]

Dr. Twelftree concludes, "Irenaeus took freedom from the demonic (in the form of evil spiritual beings needing to be expelled) to be not only the most important and common form of Christian healing but also the greatest need of the Gentiles."[60]

### Theophilus of Antioch

Theophilus of Antioch (~AD 170) was the archbishop of Antioch, whom we know little about. His understanding of spiritual warfare seemed influenced by Johannine theology, picturing universal satanic influence, not limited to lunatic demoniacs. From his point of view, demonism was not primarily expressed in insanity or physical illness but in wicked or deceived thinking, inspiring philosophers, pagans, and heretical theologians.[61] From his point of view, reasoning, logic, and sound biblical teaching were not enough to

---

59   Irenaeus of Lyons, *Against Heresies 2.31, 32.*
60   Twelftree, *In the Name of Jesus,* 252.
61   Twelftree, 254.

cure these deceived persons of their error; they needed to be delivered from the spirits that blinded them in order to be taught.

Theophilus describes a combative dialogue in exorcism, in which spirits were coerced into confessing their lies, plans, and deceptions. Through this combative dialogue, early Christians could discredit pagan gods and expose the origin of heretical doctrines.

## Johannine Christianity

Those writers we have examined, and several others, all have what we can call a "synoptic" understanding of Christianity. Their understanding of Christ and theology centered around the synoptic Gospels, focusing on actions: teaching, performing miracles, healing, and driving out demons. However, some groups and writers in the early Church seemed to have been more influenced by John's Gospel.

In some sense, John's Gospel has a different perspective on spiritual warfare and exorcism than the synoptics. For one, it does not record Jesus casting out demons. Twelftree makes the case that this absence is due to John's purpose in proving the divinity of Christ. All the miracles in John are astounding and divine in origin. Exorcisms are common and do not necessitate Christ's divinity.[62]

Despite the lack of exorcism, John's Gospel does portray spiritual warfare, clearly painting the religious authorities as demon-possessed and the offspring of Satan. Thus, Johannine theology on spiritual warfare gave a universal understanding of demonism and connected it with error. Instead of being combated with a power encounter, it must be cured with the truth.[63] The focus on truth over power encounters as a solution for demonization is reflected

---

62  Twelftree, *In the Name of Jesus*, 190–195.
63  Twelftree, 202–203.

in some early Church writings on spiritual warfare, especially those more influenced by John's writings.

## Montanus and the Charismatic Circus

By the late second century, as the canon of the New Testament was solidified and charismatic elements in Christian worship began to decline, there arose a reactionary movement called Montanism, which drastically swung against canonization and toward hyper-charismatic expression. Eusebius describes him as follows:

> There it is said that a recent convert named Montanus, while Gratus was proconsul of Syria, in his unbridled ambition to reach the top, laid himself open to the adversary, was filled with spiritual excitement and suddenly fell into a kind of a trance and unnatural ecstasy. He raved, and began to chatter and talk nonsense, prophesying in a way that conflicted with the practice of the Church handed down . . . Of those who listened at that time to his sham utterances some were annoyed, regarding him as possessed, a demoniac in the grip of a spirit of error . . . . They rebuked him and tried to stop his chatter, remembering the distinction drawn by the Lord, and His warning to guard vigilantly against the coming of false prophets. Others were elated . . . they welcomed a spirit that injured and deluded the mind and led the people astray.[64]

---

64  Eusebius, *The History of the Church*, ed. Andrew Louth, trans. G A. Williamson (London: Penguin Classics, 1989), 161.

With this, the movement began, and Montanus produced a large following, many of his disciples having similar charismatic episodes to his. The nature of the prophetic utterances was defamatory toward the Church, and eventually, Montanus and his ilk were excommunicated. The Montanists accused the orthodox Christians of being "prophet killers" due to their excommunication. Eusebius's counter was that, despite their cries of persecution, they conveniently were never bothered by Jews or Romans, giving signs of their being in league with the Devil.[65]

Having enough of this nonsense, a group of bishops confronted one of the leading prophetesses of the cult and attempted to interrogate and expel the demon from the woman while she was in a trance. However, before they could, a group of Montanist "henchmen" silenced them and prevented them from rebuking the spirit verbally.[66] In another instance with the same prophetess, an orthodox Christian confronted her and attempted to bind the spirit, but again, he, too, was thrown out by the woman's bodyguards.[67]

Eusebius describes how Montanus claimed to be the successor of several early Church prophets,[68] and that gave him authority over bishops and other leaders, despite this not being precited by the cited prophets. Further, according to Eusebius, Montanus and his female associates also were given to accept large monetary gifts and live loose, luxuriant lives, all of which pointed to their demonic inspiration.[69]

---

65  Eusebius, 162.
66  Eusebius, 163.
67  Eusebius, 167.
68  Montanus claimed to be in the tradition of Agabus and Silas of Acts, and the second-century prophets Quadratus and Ammia of Philadelphia, though their utterances and behavior were entirely dissimilar to Montanus, according to Eusebius and his sources.
69  Eusebius, 64–66.

## Summary of the Second Century

So far, throughout the second century, we can see that exorcism played a vital role in Christian ministry, along with aggressive evangelism and physical healing. Spiritual warfare, in general, definitely had a broad application, as the forces of Satan were behind most evil in the world. However, exorcism was most often applied to causes of physical illness (probably when other approaches to healing were ineffective, or demonic activity was otherwise suspected), insanity, and most commonly, heresy or erroneous thinking in various forms.

We can conclude that exorcism was common enough that Justin could cite successful Christian exorcisms as a well-known fact to his opponents. According to Irenaeus, the continually successful deliverance ministry in the Christian Church was a clear juxtaposition to heretics. Further, it appears that at least in some parts of the second-century Church, exorcism was taking place both in a missional context and within the Church of Christians.

### Philosophies of Spiritual Warfare in the Second Century Summarized

| Synoptic Philosophy on Spiritual Warfare | |
|---|---|
| Justin Martyr | Exorcism as a primary tool of evangelism and apologetics. |
| Tatian | Exorcism by prayer and fasting is necessary when dealing with mute spirits. Exorcism as a basic Christian function. |
| Irenaeus of Lyon | Exorcism as a function of evangelism, a weapon against heresy, and a test of orthodoxy. |
| Theophilus of Antioch | Demons cause heresy, and exorcism continued from the time of Christ until his pastorate at Antioch. Combative dialogue is likely. |

| Johannine Philosophy on Spiritual Warfare | |
|---|---|
| Shepherd of Hermas | Demons possess the mental real estate in Christians and unbelievers. Christians can be freed through repentance and spiritual disciplines. Exorcism proper not mentioned. |
| Ignatius of Antioch | Demonism is associated with heresy and schism in the Church. Emphasis on sanctified living patterns to combat the demonic. Exorcism proper not mentioned. |
| Letters of Barnabas | Unbelievers are possessed by demons. Conversion and the process of sanctification are the cure for demonization. |
| Athenagoras | Demonized persons who self-mutilate. Deliverance comes through conversion and the gospel. |
| Clement of Alexandria | Deliverance comes with the reception of the Truth. |

## The Third Century

By the beginning of the third century, literature and teaching on spiritual warfare began to increase, even if other charismatic expressions in the Church began to decline. The basic format and understanding of exorcism as it relates to heresy, insanity, and illness seems to solidify, and the Church seems to swing in favor of the synoptic school of thought.

## Manhandling Demons

Exorcism continued to be a major aspect of evangelism, not only in its apologetic appeal but also in private exorcisms and public power encounters. Roman historian Ramsay MacMullen asks about methods of persuasion among early Christians and concludes that most of the typical approaches to evangelism were ineffective; open-air preaching was often illegal, Christian apologetic literature wasn't widely circulated, and Christians probably had few personal evangelistic encounters as we often do today.[70] Healing miracles provided some traction because they validated the supernatural power of Christianity, but they did not necessarily disprove the other gods, who had their own reports of miracles.[71]

The most effective form of evangelism, according to MacMullen, was exorcism. His theory was that Christians were often called on for exorcism by their pagan neighbors and could effectually cure the demonization, spreading their reputation and the growth of the gospel. Exorcism was more effective than healing because Christians would "manhandle" demons, forcing them to confess their activity as hypocrite deities, beg for mercy, scream in torment, acknowledge the Lordship of Christ, and finally be expelled. MacMullen concluded that exorcism was the locomotive of evangelism and "the most highly rated activity among early Christians."[72]

Such dramatic power encounters visibly displayed the power of the Greco-Roman pantheon up against Christ, with a very clear victor. These stories would spread and lead to more requests for healing and exorcism and carried evangelism by creating more converts almost naturally. At this point, it remained incredibly effective because evangelism, healing, and exorcism were all ministries of lay persons. Any Christian could be used in this capacity and thus expand the gospel. Tertullian even confidently challenged his enemies to produce a demoniac, "and that spirit, commanded *by any Christian at all*," will confess that it is worshipped as a god, but in truth, it is nothing but a demon.[73]

---

70  MacMullen, *Christianizing the Roman Empire*, 33.
71  MacMullen, 33.
72  MacMullen, 27–28.
73  MacMullen, 27–28, emphasis mine.

With the increased use of combative dialogue, there seems to also be an increase in elements used to coerce and torment demons. Tertullian writes that Christians subdue demons by invoking "judgment fires" by laying on of hands, exsufflation (gentle blowing, to represent the Holy Spirit), and adjurations. He further writes, "The wicked spirit... will as readily make the truthful confession that he is a demon, as elsewhere he has falsely asserted that he is a god" *(Apol. 23)*. After the exorcising Christian has extracted a confession, he then forces the demon to flee, in "terror." Cyprian also described tormenting demons with "scourges" and "torturous words."[74]

Missional exorcism did, at times, take place in more public arenas and served basically the same purpose as an authentication of the gospel and humiliation of the enemy. During public power encounters, demons would likewise confess their hypocrisy and Christ's divinity. There were also imprecatory miracles, such as a false prophetess being struck dead after publicly challenging a bishop and a falsely converted Christian being called out publicly and struck with sickness.[75]

## Exorcising Temples

Exorcism was not limited to liberating the demoniac; early Church evangelists at times made a show by entering temples and exorcising the idol. If a pagan god was toppled before the name of Christ, who could honestly deny His divinity? One example is the supposed account of an apostle exorcising the Temple of Artemis. Immediately, before crowds of worshippers, the altar cracks in half.[76]

---

74    Bob Larson, International School of Exorcism, Level 1, Lesson 1.

75    MacMullen, *Christianizing the Roman Empire*, 88.

76    MacMullen, 26.

There are famous though unreliable accounts of a Christian evangelist who exemplified both these forms of warfare, namely Gregory the Wonderworker (AD 213–270). His supernatural evangelism started as he prayed in a temple overnight; in the morning, the demon of the temple told its warden that it had been expelled by Gregory. The warden finds Gregory and asks him to reinstate the spirit, and he agrees. When the warden sees how easily the evangelist overpowers the spirit, he becomes his first convert. MacMullen further recounts the exploits of Gregory:

> When Gregory was standing, teaching the people one day, behold, from among the crowd, a young man shouted out in a loud voice uttering some challenge; and Gregory exorcises the demon likewise, saying, 'Not I is it who commands you, but Christ who flung you into the sea, quit this youth!' and the demon heard the name of the divine majesty, he cried out loudly saying, 'Alas for me, for Jesus! Alas for me on account of his disciple!' . . . The devil being enraged by the territory conquered from him . . . inspired a young woman to defame him. She is a prostitute, and accuses him of being one of her lovers, but he exorcizes the evil spirits from her also."[77]

If these events are fabrications a generation or two removed from Gregory's life, they still give us a valuable understanding of what Christians understood to be taking place in and around that time. The slander and buffets against Gregory were inspired

---

77   MacMullen, 60.

by the Devil, angry at losing territory in a war over the soul(s) of the Roman Empire. As demons were exorcised, temples desecrated, and pagans converted, Satan continued to lose influence and power. The entire effort of the gospel was in conjunction with this war, and the whole goal of early Christianity was to fight and ultimately win this war until the return of Christ.

At this point, we understand that spiritual warfare took place not only on the tactical level, with conversions and exorcism, but also on the strategic level, with the Kingdom of God and the Kingdom of Darkness fighting over territory.

## Conclusions from the Early Church

The preaching of the gospel, driving out of demons, and laying of hands on the sick represented the primary, forward thrust of ministry in the early Church. The lines between these three ministries were blurry, and they were most often employed together and led to the rapid expansion of the early Church. These were primarily lay ministries. Though certain charismatic evangelists stood out, lay people probably provided the main thrust in this triad of ministry. At this time, there was not yet any office of exorcist, though the seeds of such a ministry were being planted that wouldn't come to fruition until the fourth century.

### Context of Pre-Nicene Exorcism

From what we have examined, we can see exorcism taking place in the following contexts:

1. The first and most common context was evangelism. Exorcism provided the perfect sign to combat the Greco-Roman

worldview. Belief in demons was common; therefore, when Christians exorcised demons, a pagan audience already basically understood what was taking place. The Christian would extract a confession from the demon that it had lied to its worshippers (presumably present) and that it was, in truth, a demon. This was so typical in the early Church that apologetic writers assumed their opposition was well aware of this fact. These confessions, the terrorization of demons, and the efficacy with which they were expelled were potent tools in Christian evangelism.

2. Nothing was more commonly blamed on demons than heresy. Gnostics, Montanists, and other heretics were under the influence of demonic spirits. A lack of biblical literacy or theological training may have been at play, but demonic forces only manipulated and took advantage of these factors. Because the error was demonic in source, correct teaching would not suffice to cure the heresy; the heretics had to be exorcised, and once they were dispossessed of their error, then they could receive sound teaching.

3. Exorcism was one tool employed in dealing with physical sickness and other approaches to divine healing, such as anointing or laying on of hands. Not all sickness was dealt with as demonic, but at times it certainly was. Some, such as Irenaeus and Justin, saw exorcism as the paramount form of physical healing.

4. Exorcism occurred in temples, where the idol was adjured and either cracked, fell, or ceased producing oracles.

5. Indirectly, exorcism served as an apologetic to the validity of Christianity. Christian apologists would not let their

opponents live down the public humiliation of demons, which was all too common.

For the second and third centuries, deliverance from demons was used both inside and outside the Church. Any Christian who engaged in heretical error was subject to exorcism. Montanus is a prime example, believed to be a legitimate Christian by his peers who became demonized *after* his conversion. His followers, if they returned to orthodox Christianity, were subject to exorcism before being readmitted into the Church.

For those numberless neighborhood exorcisms that drove evangelism, the ones who received deliverance were unbelievers when they were exorcised, but it is important to note that they solicited Christian exorcism. There are limited examples of demons exorcised from people who were not seeking help, though there are a handful of exceptions to this rule.

The conclusion is that the early Church exorcised Christians and unbelievers who solicited help and stood a high chance of conversion. Deliverance for uncooperative pagans was rare. Though there are some vague references to conversion as a form of deliverance from satanic bondage, there is no evidence suggesting that the early Church believed Christians could not have demons.

### Methodology of Pre-Nicene Exorcism

1. A "diagnostic combative dialogue" was essential to primitive Christian exorcism. This "manhandling" of demons served as an authentication of the gospel and a discredit to paganism. It also seems that some may have considered the demon's name and point of entry as nec-

essary to facilitate its exorcism, showing an early form of forensic deliverance.

2. Early Church exorcism was almost always public. Even the neighborhood exorcisms, which would have been in houses or private places, were "publicly" observed by friends and family. Power encounters also took place in the streets and probably in Church meetings.

3. The early Church would use forms of spiritual pressure to agitate or torment demons in order to force the demons into obedience. If a spirit was not ready to confess immediately, the Christian would invoke "judgment fire" and reminders of the foretold future of the Devil. They would employ exsufflation to cause a physical reminder of the Holy Spirit's presence, along with laying on of hands. By the third century, the signing of the cross was also used.

4. When a combative dialogue was impossible, such as in the case of a mute spirit, longer-term prayer and fasting were employed. This type of exorcism was not a matter of minutes or hours but days until God delivered the afflicted person or revealed the information necessary to facilitate the expulsion of the spirit to the ministers. Though there are some examples of this, it seems to be related to complicated cases or to mute spirits.

5. Exorcisms were fairly quick and very effective. Christian exorcism was effective enough to be sought after by unbelievers and to set it apart from heretical counterparts. There are some examples of momentary exorcisms that only took one command, such as the prostitute who challenged St. Gregory. Those who employed combative dialogue may

have had some back and forth, but they were still known for brevity and clearly delineated the authority of the Christian over the demons.

## Causation of Pre-Nicene Exorcism

The understanding and practice of deliverance among early Christians was a continuation of the commission of Christ and the practice of the apostles. Its importance grew into the third century, despite the decline of other charismatic expressions, as it was a driving factor in evangelism. The word spreading about Christianity's authority over demons and sickness continued to push Christians into confrontations with demons. It made it nearly impossible for the Church to limit it to a particular office.

The fact that the early Church understood all the pagan gods to be literal demonic spirits that were ruling the world at the behest of Satan's kingdom further drove exorcism to preeminence. Pagans worshipped and compacted with these demonic spirits. By extension, everyone outside the Church was subject to some form of demonic influence, making exorcism a spearhead of the Church. Finally, because everyone during this time had a highly spiritual worldview, exorcism was a common facet of society. The Christians' innovative, divinely empowered exorcism fit into the spiritual framework well.

## The Triad of Revival

If we consider the incredible growth of the Church within the first three centuries a "revival," which I do, then it was the most effective and sustained revival in the history of the Church. Christianity conquered the Roman Empire within three centuries and suffered only a gradual decline in fever, charisma, and zeal from the time of the apostles to the third century.

The triad of revival in the early Church combined healing, evangelism, and deliverance. The prolific and effective use of exorcism in the early Church was able to combat heresy, carry evangelism, and drive the forces of darkness back throughout the time of the early Church. It is my assessment that the prolific use of exorcism among early Christians was a major factor in their continued success in making converts and producing effective, firmly grounded Christians who were able to stand against demonism and the persecution of the Roman Empire.

CHAPTER 4

# NICENE ERA:
## EXORCISM MAINTAINS CHRISTIAN PURITY AND DOCTRINE
### AD 300-500

## The Conversion of Constantine and Nicene Christianity

A major shift took place in the Church in the fourth century during the reign of Constantine, the first Christian emperor. Until then, Christianity was fighting an uphill battle against a deeply entrenched pagan system. There were periods of hellish persecution where the Roman government sought to eradicate Christianity. Even during periods of relative tolerance, Christians were seen as atheists, backwater, uneducated, and incongruent with secular society. Christians were often blamed for natural disasters or economic depressions. All that began to change in AD 312.

With the conversion of Constantine came an officialization of Christianity as a legally recognized religion. Years after his conversion, Constantine called the First Council (AD 325) to unify Christian doctrine and establish a more cohesive Church structure and hierarchy. At this point, "primitive" Christianity became Nicene Christianity; slowly, there would be less of the supernatural and more emphasis on structure and order. Many of my protestant friends have the idea that there was a drastic shift in the Church at this time, and all the things thought to be rotten and horrible about medieval Catholicism were invented by Constantine or the council overnight. All the pagans were rounded up and baptized at sword point. However, this is not historically accurate.

The officiation of Christianity was a pivotal point in Church history; however, changes did not take place overnight. Those who lived before and during the reign of Constantine described it as a halcyon time, not the forced marriage of paganism and Christianity. Constantine and the council did not cause any immediate change in the style of worship or practice of Christians. It did change the trajectory of the Church and caused a massive influx of superficial converts.

Now that Christianity was the state religion and would grow in influence and importance throughout this period, there were many motivations to become a Christian beyond conviction. Christians filled government appointments and became the privileged class. Exorcism and other miracles were no longer the primary causes of conversion; political expediency, wealth, and societal standing became chief factors.[78]

With a massive influx of new converts, government funding, and imperial recognition, the spiritual conquest of Rome seemed to be drawing to a conclusion. Exorcism and other miracles, which were the Church's best weapons, began to decline, as now there was "peace." MacMullen records this change in landscape:

---

78  MacMullen, *Christianizing the Roman Empire*, 116–119.

Where once [Christians] had expelled devils only from poor possessed souls, now they could march in the holiest shrines and, with spectacular effect, drive the demons from their very homes . . . . Bishops now actually dined with Constantine himself; they used Constantine's palace as his headquarters. What they said now had an authority acknowledged by the Emperor himself; they hardly needed miracles to rest on. Correspondingly, fewer tales of miracles circulated.[79]

Though erosion was taking place, it was slow. Further, the driving factors were not emperors or councils but a change in motivation to become a Christian and the massive influx of paganized converts.

## Disciples or Converts?

With a change in motivations for conversion came a change in the quality of converts. Political and financial motivations for conversion created *nominal* Christians, who carried their pagan thinking with them into the Church. The Church would begin to set up guards to protect against false conversions, and initially, any incursions of pagan thinking and practices were minor. However, nominal Christians would become the majority throughout generations and greatly influence Christian culture.

An example of this influence is as follows. In the third century, Christians held martyrs in very high regard. When Christianity became recognized, Christians built monuments to these heroes

---

79 MacMullen, 113–114.

and even held feasts in remembrance of them at times. Christians believed that these saints were constantly praying in heaven for us on Earth. Someone gets healed at one of these monuments. People then associate the healing with that particular saint and begin visiting his altar. Over time, some will solicit the intercession of this saint by praying to him or her.

Over time, pagan concepts continued to slip into the Church and slowly grow in a similar manner. Though eventually, these types of thinking would come to overwhelm the Church, traditional Christianity was still defended. Now the spiritual war was not an offensive campaign of conquest but a defensive one. How long could they keep the Devil from infiltrating, splitting, or otherwise defiling the Church?

### Baptismal Exorcism

One of the most important tools the Church devolved to guard against this infiltration was baptismal exorcism. It began in the late second century, outlined in the *Apostolic Tradition*, a document that provided organizational outlines for Church practice. *Tradition* prescribed a weeklong period of repentance, examination, and exorcism for new believers before they were baptized. This process served as a real dispossession of spirits and a practical examination of converts to ensure the sincerity of their conversion.

Though baptismal exorcism was practiced in the second and third centuries, its use became mainstream and widespread in the fourth century. Its basic purpose was to prevent demons from entering the Church in new believers. Neither conversion nor baptism were sure defenses against demonization, only systematic exorcism. Church leaders were not going to wait for demons to cause heresy, division, or insanity among Christians but prevent the issues from being a problem by getting rid of the demons in the first place. In theory, if every new believer underwent exorcism, it would reduce or eliminate the need for Christians to be delivered later.

The second utility that made baptismal exorcism essential in the fourth century was *scrutiny*. The weeklong process allowed pastors to spot insincere converts, teach proper Christian doctrine, and weed out paganistic thinking. It further forced new Christians to make a very clear break from their pagan past, with detailed renunciation of their former religion.

The baptismal exorcism was a strong step away from charismatic deliverance and into aspects of forensic and ritual deliverance, though it leaned more toward ritual. It included detailed renunciations of the Devil, anointing with oil, laying on of hands, and plenty of scriptural instruction to guard new converts against heresy and filter out as much pagan thinking as possible.[80] As Christianity became mainstream, dramatic power encounters would become less common, and baptismal exorcism would become the primary form of deliverance for the Church in the post-Nicene era and would continue to be important throughout the Middle Ages and the early Reformation.

Throughout the second, third, and fourth centuries, baptismal exorcism was primarily applied to new adult converts from paganism. However, as infant baptism became more popular in the third century, it began to be applied to infants at times in a similar, more ritualized way. In this case, it was not a renunciation of demons and a past lifestyle but a cleansing of generational iniquity and

---

80  *Apostolic Tradition* 20.10.

original sin. The rite, which we will study more in the next chapter, consists of a dedication to God, a renunciation of Satan, and commands for spirits to depart from the child's life. Whatever the benefit of this practice was, it is hard to say. My estimation is that it may have provided some buffer against generational demonization at best.[81]

## Office of the Exorcist

With the massive influx of new Christians, all requiring a baptismal exorcism, regular pastors were not able to keep up. The Church began to appoint lay persons who were especially gifted in driving out demons to be "exorcists," whose primary job was to conduct these baptismal exorcisms. Despite this appointment, lay persons were still involved in non-baptismal exorcism to some degree.[82]

The secondary function of the exorcists was in the deliverance of baptized Christians. The exorcists would take in and care for severely demonized Christians, exorcising them over days, weeks, or months to deliver them from bondage. In contrast to the second century, exorcisms were now beginning to take a longer time.[83] It is noteworthy that regulations of fourth-century exorcists included baptismal exorcism and deliverance for severely bonded Christians but did not include any mention of exorcism on pagans, showing that by the late fourth century, the Church did not exorcise unbelievers, but only those who were already in the Church.

---

81  This opinion is shared by Bob Larson, interview, July 2021.

82  Patrick Toner, "Exorcist," in *The Catholic Encyclopedia*, vol. 5 (New York: Robert Appleton Company, 1909), accessed July 12, 2021, http://www.newadvent.org/cathen/05711a.htm.

83  Toner, "Exorcist."

## Ritualization of Exorcism

With the proliferation of baptismal exorcism, spiritual warfare began to be seen through a more ritualized lens. The late fourth-century exorcists were given a book of ritual baptismal exorcism that involved specific prayers, imprecations, and signs. However, even while ritual exorcism was becoming more prominent, charismatic and forensic elements still abounded at many times. Christians still employed combative dialogue, fasting, and prayer.[84] Other times, especially gifted Christians were known for driving out demons without ritual, fasting, or combative dialogue.[85]

# Continuation of Miracles According to Augustine and Chrysostom

Two of the most profound theologians of the fourth century were Augustine in the West and Chrysostom in the East, both of whom had their perspectives on spiritual warfare that add to this study.

## Augustine of Hippo

Augustine was one of the most prolific authors in Church history, producing hundreds of sermons, books, and letters. He is considered one of the great "Doctors" of Western theology; that is, persons who have greatly devolved and refined Christian thought. He is also highly respected in most protestant denominations, quoted as a trustworthy theologian by both Luther and Calvin.

Augustine understood all the Roman gods to be demons and their worshippers to be totally possessed by them; one of his main appeals to pagans in *City of God* is that Christ can set them

---

84    Toner, "Exorcist."
85    As was the case with Martin of Tours, Toner, "Exorcist."

free from the demonic power that enslaves them.[86] According to Augustine, these demons had been hard at work perverting man's thinking for centuries. Demons inspired Greek theater as a tool to spread iniquity, promoting lasciviousness in the heroic acts of the gods and heroes who were themselves perverted.[87]

In *City of God*, Augustine debunks the early attempts to establish the doctrine of cessationism. He explains that in the previous centuries, it was miracles that persuaded the known world to embrace Christianity. Still, despite Christianity having now triumphed, miracles have not ceased.[88] Throughout the rest of the book, he gives us a laundry list of miracles that he either witnessed or heard about to show that miracles were still occurring in the fourth century. Three major exorcisms are among these.

In the first case, a demonized young man near the point of death was brought to a Church meeting. When the spirits were confronted with prayers and hymns, they manifested violently:

> With a mighty shriek, the demon begged for mercy, and confessed when and where and how it made its way into the young man. Finally, it declared that it would depart from him, naming the various limbs and parts which, so it threatened, it would maim as it left them; and while saying this it withdrew from the man. But one of the eyes slipped down his jaw, hanging by a small vein from the socket... Then his brother-in-law, who was there,

---

86  Augustine, *City of God*, trans. Henry Bettenson (London: Penguin Classics, 2003), 364.

87  Augustine, 58.

88  Augustine, 1033.

said, "God who put the demon to flight has the power to restore his eye, at the prayers of his saints." He than replaced as best he could, the eye which had slipped out and was dangling there; he bound it with a napkin, and said that the bandage should not be removed for a weeks time. Those instructions were followed and his eye was found to be completely healed.[89]

Another exorcism Augustine described in *City of God* was that of a demonized virgin, who was "anointing herself with oil in which were mixed the tears of a presbyter, shed while he was praying for her" and was immediately delivered from the demon. The third example is that of a priest who prayed for a boy with a demon whom he had not met, and the boy was healed.[90]

Of these three cases, the virgin was a Christian, referring to a woman who lives a chaste life of devotion to God. The young man was probably at least a nominal Christian, as his family members who brought him to the meeting and prayed for him were believers. In the third case, there isn't evidence one way or another. In the first case, where Augustine provides the most details, there appears to have been some combative dialogue where the spirit was forced to confess its point of entry.

Though Augustine only records three exorcisms in *City of God*, he records a great number of healing miracles, including the opening of blind eyes, curing of cancers, and recovery of paralytics.[91]

---

89  Augustine, 1040.
90  Augustine, 1040.
91  Augustine, chap. 8.

This may reflect a decline in exorcism in favor of physical healing, at least in some circles.

Augustine generally saw spiritual warfare in a wide cosmological dimension, with evangelism as the primary battlefield. Contrasted with the Apostolic Fathers, exorcism seems to have moved to peripheral importance in this battle. Augustine further believed that everyone was vulnerable to demonization. He explains that our world is meant to be despised and that no one can be immune from "multifarious assaults of demons." He points out that no one can be immune from demonic attack regardless of righteousness and faith. Augustine cites the example of baptized babies of Christian parents at times tormented by demons. Though the contemporary protestant may dismiss this example, they represented the perfect example of Christian purity to Augustine, and adult Christians who are less innocent are no less immune.[92]

From Augustine's perspective, early Nicene theology supported the continuation of miracles, including exorcism in both its official ritualized form and its more charismatic forms. Further, Western Christians at this time understood that Christians were sometimes demonized and needed deliverance through actual exorcism.

### Chrysostom

Chrysostom was the archbishop of Constantinople and a highly influential theologian and preacher in the West. He is one of the greatest homilists and commentators in Church history on account of the elegance and exegesis of his sermons, most of which are preserved for us today. He is also counted as one of the great Eastern

---

92  Augustine, 1067.

Church Doctors, a foundational theologian for orthodox Christianity, and highly respected by Catholics and many protestants.

In Chrysostom's writings, one of the first aspects of spiritual warfare is his understanding of sin. Sin, from his point of view, was not just an action or behavior but a living force that needed to be actively resisted, closely related to the demonic. Exegeting Ephesians 4:26, he calls wrath an evil spirit that attempts to take up real estate in mind and emotions and must be resisted through prayer and signing the cross.[93]

Chrysostom makes it extremely clear that Christians can have demons. The question in the minds of his audience was not whether a Christian could have a demon but whether or not demons could steal someone's salvation. To Chrysostom, the answer to this question is a resounding no. Christians did have demons, but tormented Christians should not despair of their salvation. He explains, "A demon certainly will not deprive us of heaven, but doth in some cases even work with the sober-minded. But sin will assuredly cast us out. For [sin] is a demon we willingly receive, a self-chosen madness."[94]

He further warns that if Christians persist in sin, they will open themselves to demonization, and he juxtaposes the outward manifestation of a demoniac with the inward, hidden filth of sin. He explains that the ravings of demonic manifestation are outward signs of what sin looks like in the soul. After being humiliated by demonic insanity, when deliverance finally comes, the believer will be humbled and freed from both the demon and the besetting sin: "First, their being sobered and brought to more self-control; then,

---

93  Chrysostom, "Homily XXVIIL," 540.
94  Chrysostom, "Homily XLI," 254.

that having suffered here the chastisement of their own sins, they depart hence to their Master, purified."[95]

Chrysostom's understanding of Christians and demonization was influenced by the experience of a friend of his. Stagirius had fled from his home to become a monk. After entering the monastery, Stagirius became very lukewarm, and as a result of this, a demon began to torment him by causing severe fits of depression. This condition continued for a long time, and the exorcists could not deliver him. Chrysostom wrote several letters to the possessed monk, collected in three books titled *On Providence*. In these letters, he comforts and encourages the monk to trust God for his ultimate deliverance. He points out that his suffering pushed him in fasting and prayer back into a close relationship with God. He further exhorts Stagirius to reject thoughts and feelings of depression to the best of his power and encourages him to visit the sick and those in prison to be reminded he was not the only one suffering.[96]

Should Christians find themselves indwelt by demons, what is Chrysostom's advice? He doesn't speak much about exorcism, perhaps disillusioned by the impotence of those who attempted to exorcise Stagirius. He speaks more on sanctification, prayer, fasting, and resisting sin as weapons of warfare. He also spoke about confronting demons more directly through symbols of Christ, such as signing the cross. He cautions his audience against sin, and his preaching had a premium on holiness. It seems that Chrysostom's best weapon

---

95  Chrysostom, 254.
96  Alban Butler, "On the writings of St. John Chrysostom," *The Lives of the Fathers, Martyrs, and Other Principal Saints,* Vol 1 (Dublin, James Duffy, 1866; Bartleby. com, 2010), 5.

was to stay out of trouble to start with. After all, once you are in bondage, you may end up like Stagirius and never get free.

Freedom and bondage were central to Chrysostom's understanding of Christian life. When preaching on Ephesians 6, he explains that the fight is "not about riches, not about glory, but about our being enslaved." He goes on to say that Christians must stand and not win once or slay only one vice but must wage spiritual warfare continually or be subject to enslavement.[97] Chrysostom responds to some who lament this war, wishing that the Devil was totally subjected to and removed from all Christians; he calls these "insolent and slothful." He says most Christians must "wrestle" against the powers of darkness, while the apostles apparently manhandled them with a phrase or two. This is because most Christians are lazy, and if they bothered to use any power made available to them through the gospel, they would quickly find victory over both sin and demons.[98]

Though focusing more on combating the deadly force of sin, Chrysostom does give us some insight into exorcism that took place in his day. When commenting on Acts 19, he explains that the demon needed to recognize Christ and Paul before pulverizing the Jewish exorcists; the demons were always forced to revere Christ publicly and confirm his gospel, otherwise, they would suffer wrath. "But observe how we find the demons everywhere more right minded (than the Jews), not daring to contradict nor accuse the Apostles, or Christ."[99]

From Chrysostom's writings, we can see that forth-century Eastern Christians were still practicing exorcism and that they believed

---

97   Chrysostom, "Homily XLI," 160.
98   Chrysostom, 161.
99   Chrysostom, 254.

Christians could have demons. These exorcisms seemed to have had a decline in effectiveness, as demonized Christians were not able to be delivered simply, but at times had to endure long periods of suffering, if they were delivered at all. As these exorcisms became more ritualized, they also became less effective. Spiritual disciplines like prayer, fasting, and contrite repentance could be used to prevent demonization, or weaken their influence, if already present.

## Conclusions

In the fourth century, Christianity underwent some serious changes. Despite a general decline in charismatic expression since the late second century, exorcism managed to remain a regular part of Christian life, though in an increasingly ritualized form. Spiritual warfare remained a major part of the Christian experience, but its understanding and practice had some variations from the previous centuries.

### Context of Nicene Exorcism

In the post-Nicene era, some changes began to take place in the context in which exorcism was happening:

1. Exorcism as a response to heresy continued to happen, though it began to decline after AD 312.
2. Exorcism as a response to physical sickness also declined after AD 312. More sporadic miracles, in response to intercession or laying on of hands, seem to be the more prominent forms of healing.
3. Baptism became the primary context of exorcism. This was believed to be a real exorcism with real demons being

expelled, but one of its main utilities was to scrutinize new believers and determine their authenticity. It also provided a place to discover, challenge, and finally correct wrong doctrines in new converts and hopefully purge new converts of their pagan beliefs along with their pagan demons. This became the most common form of exorcism at this time and would continue to be the dominant form of exorcism throughout the Middle Ages.

4. Mental illness, which was a secondary form of demonization to early Christians, became a primary type in the Nicene era. Persons who were actually insane, or experiencing demoniac manifestations at all times, never being in their right mind, were classified as "energumen." Christians who were baptized and exorcised at conversion and later developed this condition were most often the persons exorcised.

5. *Mental illness* in a milder form, such as severe anxiety or depression, such as the case of Stagirius, was also addressed with exorcism. This type of bondage was milder than would require classification as energumen but was still considered a form of demonization.

Officially designated exorcists began to appear during this time, who primarily took the helm of exorcism, though lay persons and other clergy were sometimes still casting out demons. Exorcists were chosen not based on ordination but on gifting and charismatic power. The delineation of exorcists from other clergy and laity became more concise as time passed, until eventually, the laity would be completely excluded from exorcism in the following centuries.

By this point in history, it seems that exorcism on pagans was very rare. Instructions for fourth-century exorcists included various contexts in which exorcism should take place, and all of those contexts are on Christians with no mention of unbelievers. Exorcists are instructed to minister to two groups: Christians who have been baptized and the catechumen, a Christian who is about to be baptized. Further, in at least the writings of Chrysostom and Augustine, it is clear that they believed Christians had demons.

As the Church became more politically dominant, the need to assert authority with the supernatural became less important. By the fifth century, exorcism was on a sharp decline, surviving primarily through infantile baptismal exorcism. Some Christians may have understood the great spiritual war to be closing, with the conversion of Europe and with a decline in paganism; to them, it made sense that exorcism wasn't as important.

## Methodology of Exorcism

In the fourth and fifth centuries, exorcism was becoming less charismatic. There were some more forensic elements, but it moved primarily toward ritual exorcism. The following are the major changes:

1. Apotaxis, or the renunciation of the Devil, became a common and important part of exorcism; its use is especially highlighted in baptismal exorcism. Confession from past sins and detailed renunciations of vows, covenants, and dedications became an important part of baptismal exorcism as a way of systemically and fully surrendering oneself to Christ.

2. Specific formulas were used in a similar manner to pagan and Jewish exorcism. This involved recitation of the rite along with form prayers and acts that would accompany the rite. According to *New Advent*, the rite of exorcism prescribed by the Fourth Council of Carthage is preserved in *Pontificale Romanum*, a Catholic liturgical manual.

3. Laying on of hands became an important and common feature of exorcism throughout this time. It was emphasized in baptismal exorcism, which climaxed with the bishop laying hands on the candidate and exorcising him,[100] and in the exorcism rite, where the exorcist was commanded to memorize the formula and utilize it through "imposing" hands on the demonized.

4. A combative dialogue was still employed at times.

5. Exorcism by prayer and fasting appears more regularly here. St. Martin is said to have regularly employed this method, without laying on of hands or use of formula, with some degree of success. The third exorcism cited by Augustine also sees a Christian exorcise a demon by prayer, without ever having met the victim.

6. Exorcism took place more often in a controlled environment when compared to the early Church. With the officialization of exorcists and written procedures of exorcism, it is easy to see how it became more frequent an activity on the inside of a church than on the streets and in the open. Since Christianity was officially adopted, people who wanted help from demons would more likely go to a church building than have a house call.

---

100 *Apostolic Tradition* 20.4.

7. Exorcisms were becoming longer and less effective. Demonized persons needed to be housed, fed, and taken care of while exorcists attempted to free them.
8. Like the early Church, the Nicene Church used spiritual pressure to torment demons in the process of exorcism. However, these forms of pressure appear to be different and include elements such as anointing with oil, signing the cross, exsufflation, and possibly holy water by the fifth century.

Evangelism was still considered a high form of spiritual warfare. All pagans are assumed to be demonized as they worship demons, a point consistently brought up by Christian apologists. As souls were converted and pagans turned to Christ, the Devil further lost territory. Pagans were called to help defeat the Devil by turning toward Christ. The very action of conversion was damage done to the kingdom of Satan.

Spiritual warfare was seen as the daily, universal battle of the Christian against sin through the process of sanctification. The relationship between sin and the Devil was emphasized by the Church Doctors. Sin was very often spoken of as a "he" rather than an "it." This personification of sin as a living being temping to transgression emphasized its force and strength beyond a mere choice of right and wrong. The daily battle to grow in virtue and to decrease in vice was a form of spiritual warfare.

## Factors of Change

The officialization of Christianity was the pivotal change in this period. A gradual move toward ritualism and away from charisma was already taking place beforehand but was increased during this period. With the general unification and organization of Christianity, exorcism was also affected, becoming more organized and controlled. With the increase of systematic theology also came a more defined theology about spiritual warfare as well.

The changes in need also greatly shaped spiritual warfare during this period. Exorcism was no longer needed as a fundamental part of evangelism. However, it adopted a new role as screening for new believers during the baptismal process and would continue to be used on Christians suffering from mental illness. With a high influx of converts, baptismal exorcism needed to be done quickly and efficiently, leading to changes in practice.

## Slowing of Decline?

By the late fourth century, the Church was not experiencing the same degree of charismatic revival fervor as in its infancy. Eventually, the Church would become more attached to the State and would become the Roman Catholic Church of the Middle Ages. Did the practice of exorcism in the Nicene era serve any good, seeing this decline?

My analysis is that the practice of baptismal exorcism did serve to slow the rate of decline in the Nicene Church. At the least, it served as a time for new believers to receive instruction in Christian doctrine and to discard some of their pagan styles of thinking. In its early use, it's possible it did provide some actual spiritual traction, freeing some new believers from demonic strongholds and reducing the number of demonic problems in the Church.

The exorcism of mentally ill Christians seems to have lost its luster and was becoming less effective. How this affected spiritual warfare, in general, is difficult to say. At best, it brought relief to those suffering from demonic problems, but it doesn't seem to have affected evangelism or the life of the Church much. The reduction of the ministry to an order of exorcists and away from laity no doubt reduced the ability of exorcism to be used as a powerhouse for evangelism. Ironically, as specific training, knowledge, and officiation were passed down, exorcisms took longer and produced fewer results. One might further question how.

Even though the spiritual warfare of the Nicene Church Doctors emphasized the relationship between sin and the Devil, Christians could undergo systematic spiritual housecleaning at their baptism and later on become so tormented by demons that they were classified as energumen; it could take days to months to deliver them, if at all. If these cases were demonization and not mental illness, it seems the Order of Exorcists was dropping the ball.

Though the decline was checked early on by good theologians and systematic practice of spiritual warfare, it wasn't stopped. As exorcism became less effective and less common outside of baptism, more nominal Christians would enter the Church and become the majority. Pagan influences would slowly gain prominence, and the Church would decline into the Dark Ages.

CHAPTER 5

# THE MEDIEVAL ERA:
## THE DEATH OF DELIVERANCE AND THE BIRTH OF SACRAMENTAL EXORCISM
### AD 500-1517

T he Middle Ages and their aura of superstition, religion, and spirituality are often considered a time ripe with exorcism, though this assumption couldn't be further from the truth. Historian Francis Young calls this period a time of "profound crises" for spiritual warfare.[101] We will find that exorcism in the broadest sense flourished from the apostolic time to about the late fourth century, began a slow decline that climaxed in its near extinction in the High Middle Ages, and had a rebirth in the late Middle Ages, though in an entirely different form, the earliest form of the contemporary Catholic rite of exorcism. Baptismal exorcism, briefly covered in the previous chapter, would be the most significant and enduring form of spiritual warfare practiced by the Church

---

101 Francis Young, *A History of Exorcism in Catholic Christianity* (Cambridge: Palgrave Macmillan, 2016), 26.

between Nicaea and the Reformation, and it will be given a more thorough examination in this chapter.

## Christendom and Its Implications for Spiritual Warfare

By the sixth century, pagan influence was marginal in Europe and shrinking fast. A universal, Roman-style Christian Church was nearly homogeneous throughout European societies. As much as civil authority was able to displace the need for the supernatural, it also replaced the need for evangelism and missions. Though missions did sometimes take place, the expansionary force of Christianity changed from the power of God to the point of the sword.

In this homogeneous Christian society, conversion and faith in Christ was not understood as it is today. A Christian was any member of society who was baptized, and every member of the community was a Church member as well. Heathens need not have a "born again" experience but simply acknowledge the supremacy of Christ and receive baptism. Salvation was not as much a reflection of a relationship with Christ but participation in sacraments and membership of the universal Church.

Because of this shift in the concepts of conversion and evangelism, which had been taking place since the time of Augustine, the evangelistic zeal of the early days began to evaporate. The work of ministry shifted firmly away from laity into the hands of ordained ministers, who would lead the societal Church in teaching and participation in sacraments.

Evangelistic spiritual warfare thus became a civil matter. There was, at times, a concept of fighting back against immorality and converting (or subjugating) unbelievers, but this became the work of civil authority to punish wrongdoers and to fight against heathen or Muslim nations. As far as nominal Christians within Christendom, salvation was not a matter of experiencing conversion or repentance but a daily battle of sanctification and appropriating God's grace. Though this may have encouraged people to live righteously in theory, it left no place for evangelism in the minds of lay people.

Because evangelism suffered a fatal blow to its value, authenticating miracles of healing and exorcism suffered also. There are stories of miracles, including healing and exorcism, which took place during the Middle Ages, but many stories of the supernatural took on a different flavor than that of the early Church, as Christianity absorbed the Greco-Roman and eventually Germanic cultures of its host nations.

## Shift to Baptismal Exorcism

By the fifth century, there was little literature about casting out demons. There was no real doctrinal shift when compared to the previous century; no new doctrine that reclassified or understood exorcism. Belief about it did not change, or it didn't appear to change; however, it seems that it became less frequent. One explanation put forth by MacMullen and echoed by many protestants is that after Constantine was converted in AD 312, the Church no longer leaned on miracles for its survival; it didn't need the power of God since it was now backed by the power of the State.[102] This decline of the supernatural reached its near conclusion by the sixth century. With the Church firmly replacing the power vacuum left by Rome, strong civil authority left no need for supernatural evangelism.

---

102 MacMullen, *Christianizing the Roman Empire*, 113.

The Catholic Church, which has always maintained a belief in exorcism, believes it is not because of lack of interest, but a decrease in the influence of the Devil. Rev. Michael Moore is a Catholic priest and a deliverance minister.[103] He explained to me in an interview that as Christianity became dominant during the Middle Ages, demonization was much less frequent, seeing as how people were not worshipping demons through pagan sacrifices and witchcraft. He also believes that baptismal exorcism severely eroded satanic influence over the generations it had been practiced. These factors left very little need for exorcism on adult Christians.

That being said, one way spiritual warfare was steadfastly maintained was through baptismal exorcism. Linards Jansons, Doctor of Ministry and long-standing Lutheran pastor, explains that, while exorcism may seem exotic to us today, "the fact is, most Christians throughout most of history went through exorcism at least once—at the font."[104] He goes on to describe the original form of baptismal exorcism as a complex process that could last months, or even years, if the catechumenate so elected to delay the baptism. (At the time, baptism was understood to be the moment at which sins were washed away, and post-baptismal sin carried a much greater weight, hence the elected delay.) Renunciation of Satan, called apotaxis, was one of the oldest and most central aspects of these

---

103 The Catholic Church holds that there are various degrees of demonization and an approach to deal with each degree. "Exorcism" in Catholic terminology is a rite employed only for the most severe and valid cases of demonization, and exorcists are those qualified to perform this rite. "Deliverance short of exorcism" can involved a number of prayers or exorcistic tactics to cure demonization. Rev. Moore is *not* a Catholic exorcist, but he does regularly engage in "deliverance short of exorcism," which, based on his description, is very similar to contemporary protestant deliverance ministries.

104 Linards Jansons, "Baptismal Exorcism: An Exercise in Liturgical Theology," *Lutheran Theological Journal* 45, no. 3 (December 2011): 183–97.

pre-baptismal exorcisms. These renunciations were not general or vague but very specific, including the previous life's gods, sins, rites, and vows. Even physical actions were used to display this breaking of ties with Satan. After the renunciations, exorcism, and baptism, statements of allegiance to Christ were made to juxtapose the apotaxis; these statements were separate from the apostle's creed and were called syntaxis.[105]

After the apotaxis, anointing began to play a "dominant" role in baptismal exorcisms. In the earliest rites, before the exorcistic elements were added, anointing with oil was still important as a symbol of the Holy Spirit. As baptismal exorcism began to become ritualized, anointing with oil became the touch point of expulsion for the Devil. The oil represented a spiritual conductor of sorts and a touch point of faith for the infilling of the Holy Spirit and the expulsion of demons. After the conclusion of the baptism, the candidate was anointed again, this time for protection and sealing. These post-baptismal anointings also prevented the re-entry of deposed demons, so specific anointings were used to seal the eyes, ears, or whatever other point the demons may have entered.

Another common element in baptismal exorcism was *exsufflation*, a gentle breathing out by the baptizer on the candidate. Jansons explains this "symbolised contempt for the devil... but [also] a gentle blowing of the Holy Spirit."[106] These elements, along with the progressive adaptation of holy water, crucifixes, salt, etc., began to give rise to the number of elements seen in modern Catholic exorcism. The use of these various elements was not uniform

---

105 Jansons, 3.
106 Jansons, 2.

throughout all baptismal exorcisms,[107] or other exorcisms, but was increasingly common and gave the foundation for a rite of exorcism to be uniformly established in Catholicism.

As stated earlier, baptismal exorcism was codified in the document *Apostolic Tradition*, which started in the third century. Into the fourth and fifth centuries, as the Roman Empire adopted Christianity, a vast number of converts began coming to the Church, and the interest in vetting baptismal candidates became more important. With thousands of pagans flocking to the font, the Church needed to ensure that these new converts would be fully Christianized. Along with exorcism, this vetting period was also used to indoctrinate new converts so that they fully understood what becoming a Christian was about.[108]

By the seventh century, baptismal exorcism was becoming fairly uniform. Jansons creates a list of the elements and order of baptismal exorcism by cross-referencing several documents from the period:

- "enrolment in the catechumenate for an unspecified period of time, with rites such as giving of blessed salt, followed by a period of instruction with frequent exorcisms (the scrutinies)
- election to baptism, with a final period of election comprising the 40 days of Lent
- three scrutinies on the 3rd, 4th and 5th Sundays of Lent
- pre-baptismal anointing of the senses, which served both to seal the word of God in the candidate and to fortify them from further corruption

---

107 Jansons, 2.
108 Jansons, 6.

- baptism by triple emersion
- vesture in white
- first post-baptismal anointing by presbyter (signifying assimilation to priesthood of Christ)
- second post-baptismal anointing by bishop (signifying the reception of the Holy Spirit—the origin of the later sacrament of 'confirmation')
- reception of baptismal eucharist, including (for this time only) milk and honey"[109]

Note the terms for scrutiny and exorcism are interchangeable in the historical documents. The exorcisms sought to expel demonic spirits but also served as a test for conversion legitimacy. The administrators had some way of exposing false converts and setting them aside, though exactly what tools were used is unclear. It is possible that certain demonic reactions, or a spirit admitting that their host's faith was incomplete, were part of this if the diagnostic dialogue from the previous centuries was preserved up until this point.

In addition, we see the prototype for the rite of confirmation. In accounts in Acts, baptism in water and the reception of the Holy Spirit are two separate events. The preservation of this tradition is found here, with the anointing of the bishop for the reception of the Holy Spirit. As mentioned, this would eventually evolve to be a separate rite in liturgical denominations. At the advent of the Pentecostal movement in the twentieth century, it would become understood as "the Baptism of the Holy Spirit," which has the same theological concept with widely differing applications.

---

109 Jansons, 6.

Soon, most candidates were not ex-pagan adults but the infant children of Christian families. Initially, all the same complexity for adult converts would be applied to the infants, with parents speaking renunciations on behalf of the child. However, over time, Jansons explains that the rite became "compressed, or 'telescoped,' into a shorter and shorter time period."[110] This is an understandable reaction for two reasons. Firstly, the complexity of the process for adults was retained because the system was likely successful in provoking demonic reactions, exposing sins, and filtering out false converts. None of these were possible with infants, so all the details would have been superfluous. Secondly, the concept that satanic influence could be eroded, not just in an individual's life, but throughout a culture and a society, as generations passed off successfully cleansed blood, the need for deeper cleansing became less. Baptismal exorcism was no longer a corrective maintenance but a preventive one.

Looking at baptismal exorcism, though it may seem exotic to us today, it was, in its heyday, a vastly important rite in Christianity. It was a way of making the Church "bulletproof," so to speak. If demonic forces were stopped at conversion or shortly after birth, it kept Satan from influencing the inside of the Church, provided post-baptism Christians maintained resilient faith. Of course, this system wasn't foolproof, as the occasional demoniac and classical exorcism occurred during this time, though markedly less frequently than in the pre-Nicene era.

These rites were not simply a ritual, as we would consider today's terms. They were considered to hold practical purposes. They sought

---

110  Jansons, 6.

to involve and indoctrinate the candidate in the word of God; every command or rebuke was riddled with scripture. This process helped welcome new converts into the Church—these long seasons of repentance and examination were public, involving the rest of the Church. These countless hours likely included fellowship; it was a time when new believers and congregants got to know each other.

Most importantly, though, Jansons points out, "it was believed that something really *happened* as a result of the rite: demons were actually cast out, then and there."[111] Therefore, it was anything but pure symbolism, at least at first. The aforementioned benefits were only secondary to the primary purpose of an exorcism, to cast out demons. However, these other aspects reflect a wider view of spiritual warfare. Liberation from demonic power was only the beginning; new believers were trained in how to resist Satan throughout the remainder of their life. Understanding the Word, being filled with the Holy Spirit, and being connected to the Church were all vital to the continuation of freedom in Christ.

Baptismal exorcism also reflected a growing belief in the continuation of salvation, that someone's conversion was not when they were "saved" but the beginning of a process of salvation that would be completed in heaven. The long process of baptismal exorcism reflected the process of sanctification, which was a lifetime process. It also strongly reflected the doctrine of original sin, especially with the exorcism of infants. This doctrine put forth the idea that every human being was guilty of sin from Adam and shared in the guilt of the sin of their forefathers since Adam. This doctrine is well articulated by Augustine in *City of God*:

---

111 Jansons, 11

... man was willingly perverted and justly condemned, and so begot perverted and condemned offspring. For we were all in that one man [Adam], seeing that we all were that one man who fell into sin through the woman who was made from him before the first sin. We did not yet possess forms individually created and assigned to us for us to live in them as individuals; but there already existed the seminal nature from which we were to be begotten. And of course, when this was vitiated through sin, and bound with death's fetters in its just condemnation, man could not be born of man in any other condition.[112]

It was understood that the sin and iniquity of the parents would naturally be present in the offspring unless something was done to neutralize it; baptismal exorcism was a way of ensuring children started off with a clean slate so to speak.

## The Death of Deliverance and Birth of Rite

Despite baptismal exorcism maintaining its importance throughout the Middle Ages, the classic exorcism of adults did not enjoy the same protection.

Starting in the fourth century, exorcism began a gradual shift toward ritualization. It was once firmly in the hands of any lay Christian who could effectively drive out demons. In fact, those who were officially designated as exorcists were forbidden ordination; the thought that their ability to exorcise demons rested on faith and not on office.[113] The ability to perform exorcisms became

---

112 Augustine, *City of God*, 523.
113 Young, *History of Exorcism in Catholic Christianity*, 40.

more restricted over time and became "the preserve of holy individuals."[114] This restriction continued, and by the sixth century, not even priests or exorcists could diagnose demonization without the bishop's permission.[115]

As exorcism became more restricted, it decreased in use. Adult Christian exorcism became less frequent until it was scarce by the eighth century. It was rarely used in a missional setting, except for the evangelism of Northern Europe, where it was used in an increasingly magical and ritualized form adapted to the culture of Germanic paganism.[116] Exorcists on the frontiers of Christendom began to invoke a litany of names, including numerous names of God, angels, and saints, especially those who had local cult followings.[117]

Exorcism began to become less associated with the actions of an exorcist and more connected with objects and holy places. The exorcism of objects came into practice in the West by the late fourth century; it was believed that objects were corrupted because of the fall, and an exorcistic invocation over them restored them to an Edenic condition, proper for use in ceremony. This was most common with water and salt, which could be used in baptism, exorcism proper, or other ritual uses.[118]

As exorcism petered out of the medieval Church, it became something like trivial household magic. Exorcism incantations were used to chase away bees, headaches, and bad eyesight, with very

114 Young, 28.
115 Young, 45.
116 Young, 57.
117 Young, 57.
118 Young, 39.

little real confrontation with demons.[119] As it became akin to folk magic, it was abandoned by High Churchmen and theologians.

As the High Middle Ages approached, exorcism and exorcists disappeared from literature. Whisps of spiritual warfare remained in stories of demoniacs seeking deliverance at the shrines of saints and with the use of relics. By the thirteenth century, there was virtually no record of it.[120] As Christianity became dominant in Europe, there were no major enemies to demonize and no use for exorcism beyond a vague association with the conversion of pagans on the frontiers of Christendom. With the slow death of charismatic exorcism and even regular ritual exorcism, demonized persons were often left without help, and thrown out of churches, often for clerics' lack of confidence in or understanding of exorcism.[121]

Toward the end of the High Middle Ages and into the late Middle Ages, heresy and witchcraft began to make a comeback. At certain periods in the early and High Middle Ages, there was skepticism about whether witchcraft really existed at all. The stereotype of witch hunts only came into being toward the end of this period. With these new enemies, the Church went to drag exorcism out of its grave in order to fight these new threats.

This return of exorcism, severed from its connection to the primitive and Nicene Churches, took on an entirely new form: high ritual. The crude, trivial, and magical exorcism forms that existed from the twelfth and thirteenth centuries were refined and professionalized.[122] The Church reorganized professional exorcists,

119 Young, 69.
120 Young, 62.
121 Young, 82.
122 Young, 76.

no longer charismatic laymen, but educated, trained, and ordained churchmen. As the Host of Hell began to rise, the medieval Church recalled their lost reserves. By the fifteenth century, ritual exorcism was far from centralized, but systematic exorcism manuals began to appear, including rites for exorcism proper and other warfare-type prayers.[123] These systems and rites would eventually be further refined, processed, and brought together into the *Rituale Romanum*, which would become the official Catholic exorcism manual in the early Reformation and has remained largely similar until today.

Even as exorcism was being professionalized, it still had a confused air about it, with many late medieval exorcists using nonsensical tactics such as manhandling the persons undergoing exorcism as if that somehow hurt the demons.[124]

As exorcism made a resurgence in primarily liturgical forms, it did make a comeback in some rare instances of forensic and charismatic exorcism. Hildegard's exorcisms are one example cited by Young. She delivered through "empirical observation" and employed tactics such as combative diagnostic dialogue, interrogation, repentance, and revelations from the Holy Spirit.[125] However, these sorts of expressions were rare and came out of use in favor of the more ritualized forms of exorcism that became dominant into the sixteenth century.

## Conclusions

Exorcism had a major decline throughout the Middle Ages in frequency and effectiveness. It remained strongest in an increasingly

---

123 Young, 76.
124 Young, 78.
125 Young, 78.

ritual and simplified baptismal exorcism. Beyond baptism, exorcism was related to the conversion of pagans at the beginning of the period. Toward the middle of the decline, it became a trivial household incantation. As exorcism was revived, it was more related to combating magicians, witches, and heretics and itself resembled more magic than the exorcisms of Christ.

As exorcism declined, its most trivial forms were practiced by lay persons, though exorcism proper was primarily used by priests and exorcists when they were in operation. There were exceptions to this, as especially saintly people were occasionally involved in exorcism. Otherwise, exorcism became increasingly the territory of specially trained clergy by the end of the period.

## Did Medieval Christians Have Demons?

The question of Christians having demons was not a problem for medieval Christians, who understood salvation differently from most of us. Medieval Catholicism understood salvation as a process that began at conversion. However, nothing in their theology conflicted with baptized and even righteous Christians being demonized.

## Causation and Style of Medieval Exorcism

The State Church was a significant factor in the decline of exorcism's use. The homogeny of Christian society, lacking visible threats, also probably contributed to its decline. The increasingly ritualized and less effective forms of exorcism also probably became less appealing. If it didn't provide any visible utility, and it didn't work very well when it was employed, it is understandable why it wasn't very popular. The revival of exorcism at the end of the fourteenth century was contributed to by a return of visible enemies of the Church, found in heretics and witchcraft. However, this revived form was much more ritualized and systematic.

The forms of exorcism varied widely, ranging from something akin to folk magic in the early Middle Ages and something closer to high liturgy in the late period. In all cases, exorcism, when used, was considerably less effective than it had been in the periods of the first two chapters. There were certain rare situations in the late Middle Ages where exorcists employed some forensic tactics, such as interrogation, repentance, divine revelation, etc. However, even in these cases, the exorcisms were primarily ritual.

## The Church in Decline

In concluding on the effects of medieval spiritual warfare, it is clear that societal homogeny, moral decline, and a decline in the importance of exorcism are interrelated factors. Biblical exorcism declined steadily, grew in liturgical trappings, and moved out of the public Church life, surviving in missions and monasteries until nothing was left. Deliverance died in the High Middle Ages, and when it was reanimated, it shared more similarities with the work of magicians than it did with the ministry of Christ. Without an active, biblical ministry of exorcism, the Devil slipped in, slowly building his stronghold in the Church undetected.

CHAPTER 6

# THE PROTESTANT REFORMATION:
## EXORCISM RESTORED AND REDACTED
### AD 1517–1700

## Spiritual Warfare for Early Reformers

The first generation of protestant reformers were primarily concerned with purifying the Church from tradition and Greco-Roman influences, and to them, this was a spiritual battle. Reformers had no concept of creating a new Church or denomination. They believed that when false doctrine and practice were exposed, and reforms were put in place, the entire Church would eventually succumb to the Reformation and purify itself of extra-biblical traditions. They maintained a vision of a universal Church united under a single confession of faith. At the time, this idea wasn't far-fetched. In the past, Church councils were called, doctrines reviewed, understandings amended, and reforms implemented. But the Church always remained united.

Reformers believed that the true gospel had been buried beneath centuries of tradition, and the goal was to uncover it. Once unearthed, the gospel would reform the Church itself. Though demon possession and exorcism were a part of Luther's framework, the primary thrust of spiritual warfare was in the reformation of the Church, not deliverance of the bound. Despite that focus, the sixteenth and seventeenth centuries would probably have more talk and practice of exorcism than any other point between Nicaea and Azusa Street.

## The Protestant Reaction to Catholic Ritual Exorcism

During the time of the Reformation, exorcism would be used as a tool to promote the agendas of both Catholics and reformers, both sides attempting to "manhandle demons," and force them to show how demonic the other side was, in a similar way the early Church used exorcism to discredit paganism. However, over time, Catholic exorcism would become so obnoxious that protestants would distance themselves from any involvement in casting out demons.

Some Catholic exorcisms went so far as to be staged by exorcists to promote the Catholic Church. One such example was that of adolescent Nicole Aubry, which took place between 1565 and 1566. The girl was exorcised daily at first at a village church. The special became so popular that she was paraded to the cathedral in Laon. There, during her exorcisms, she would call out the secret sins of onlookers and respond to questions in Latin. Finally, the priest discovered that the demon that possessed her was Beelzebub, the leader of the French Huguenots.[126]

---

126 Young, *History of Exorcism in Catholic Christianity*, 106.

These sorts of scenes became more common; protestants and less superstitious Catholics became weary of the concept of exorcism altogether. The prominent sixteenth-century Catholic theologian Erasmus wrote a satirical critique of this superstitious sentiment in a work called *The Specter*, where a man convinces a priest that the church graveyard was haunted by souls in purgatory by using trickery. The work intended to combat superstition among Catholics but ended up amplifying the sentiment among protestants that exorcism was nothing but a magic trick.

To be sure, the type of exorcism practiced by sixteenth-century Catholics was more superstitious than biblical and was rightly criticized by protestants. However, the association between spiritual warfare and "popish magic" would be a difficult hurdle to overcome and would work to extinguish any legitimate, biblical exorcism among protestants.

## Debate over Baptismal Exorcism

The Reformed branch of Protestantism began to come into conflict with Luther over the nature of the Lord's Supper. Luther declared that the host and wine were the body and blood of Christ in a literal sense while also not losing their properties as bread and wine, a slight step away from transubstantiation. He further taught that the sacrament imputed faith and grace to the recipient. Zwingli vehemently denied both, declaring that communion was only symbolic and an act of remembrance with no further spiritual significance.[127]

When Luther and Zwingli tried to reconcile, their debate fell apart into heated exchanges. From then on, Reformed Christianity

---

127 Roger E. Olson, *The Story of Christian Theology: Twenty Centuries of Tradition and Reform* (Downers Grove, IL: IVP Academic, 1999), 404–7.

took a stronger turn away from many traditions that Lutherans sought to retain, such as Church art, candles, and various aspects of the liturgy. These differences began to form a large rift in the Reformation. The most important center of conflict for this study is the controversy of baptismal exorcism.

In the last fifteen centuries, the exorcism tradition of Christ slowly declined until disappearing almost entirely in the High Middle Ages. The exorcism tradition that returned to take its place was not connected with that of the Gospels or the early Church but was purely ritual exorcism. This style of exorcism was not compatible with either branch of protestantism. However, Lutheran and Reformed responses to the subject differed, and that conflict would manifest itself over baptismal exorcism.

Lutherans taught that the prayers of baptismal exorcism (modified from their Catholic predecessor) could break any demonic power off the infant. However, that was not the major issue. The theological implications were far more important. Baptismal exorcism inherently acknowledged original sin, the reality of exorcism, and the necessity of deliverance for Christians. Calvinists took issue with this, being deeply unsettled by the idea of the children of Christian parents having demons. Therefore, they accused Lutherans of being Catholic magicians in reformers' robes.[128]

The controversy came to a head when princes in Germany came under the influence of Calvinistic teaching. Its first eruption was in the province of Thuringia, where a Lutheran pastor deviated from using the rite of baptism, despite his supervisor's instructions, accus-

---

128  Bodo Nischan, "The Exorcism Controversy and Baptism in the Late Reformation," *Sixteenth Century Journal* 18, no. 1 (1987), https://www.jstor.org/stable/2540628.

ing those who did perform the rite of being magicians. The region's bishop began accusing the detractor of being a closet Anabaptist. The matter only ended when the junior pastor was banished.[129]

The matter continued to spread through Germany as various noblemen and princes took sides, and pastors began preaching and publishing polemics supporting their respective side. In 1591, the Prince of Saxony issued an edict that outlawed exorcism in his province in violation of his previous promise to his clergymen. Those pastors who did not obey were imprisoned. Lutherans began to fire back at various pro-Calvinist leaders, saying that their real goal was not to eliminate exorcism but to engulf Lutheranism altogether. Supporters of exorcism began to threaten violence if the rite was not restored.[130]

The fight teetered back and forth for several more years; whenever one side came to power again, it would imprison proponents of the other or banish them. Though Calvinists never gained control in Germany, exorcism would eventually fall into disuse, even among the most orthodox Lutherans. Between the efforts of Calvinists, the increasingly magical practices of Catholics, and the incoming influence of the Enlightenment, baptismal exorcism was abandoned by Lutherans for good.

Though baptismal exorcism, even in its modified Lutheran form, was highly ritualized, its removal was most significant for the theological implications. The removal also led to the removal of the general practice of casting out demons and the understanding of the demonization of Christians, both of which would become more unpopular due to this controversy.

129 Nischan, 32–34.
130 Nischan, 38–40.

## The Recovery of Missions and Evangelism

A thousand years of a homogeneous and nominal Christian society put evangelism out of business. The first generation of protestants sought to reform the Church and bring it back to a more biblical model. Still, that effort fell apart as protestant denominations split up, and the Catholic Church signed the divorce papers at the Council of Trent. There would be no unified Church, Reformed or Catholic.

The result of this split led second- and third-generation protestants to descend from spiritual fever into a cold, mean, and intransigent orthodoxy. Each camp created exhaustive theological statements of faith and lambasted the other groups who were far too foolish to see things the right way. This took place between Catholics and protestants as well as various protestant groups. This culture of valuing right doctrine began to neglect concern for right living or any sort of Christian experience beyond adherence to a set of beliefs.[131]

Out of this environment was born the backlash of Pietism. Some forms of Pietism began to stir very shortly after the icicle theologians took over; however, it was consummated by Count von Zinzendorf and the Moravians. They did not dismiss Orthodox doctrine completely but valued a moral life and lively religious experience over "dead orthodoxy." The outflow of cultivating a real relationship with Christ birthed a desire to preach the gospel to the world. Thus, the Moravians were the first to reignite a missional mindset since the earlier centuries of the Church.[132]

---

131  Olson, *Story of Christian Theology*, 445.
132  Bruce L. Shelley, *Church History in Plain Language*, 4th ed. (Nashville, TN: Thomas Nelson, 2013), 343.

As Zinzendorf and the Pietists began to restore the lifestyle of lively Christianity, Jacob Arminius restored a theology that better supported evangelism. The second-generation protestants upheld increasingly stronger versions of predestination as the only biblical view of salvation and any alternative as Catholic heresy. Olson explains, "They believed that salvation can only be a sheer gift... if the human person is totally passive in regeneration, conversion and justification," therefore, humans can have no will or decision in that justification, one way or the other. Hence, people were either elected or damned. On the other hand, Arminius taught that people needed to be presented with the gospel and either accept it or reject it.[133] Though Calvinists today will more often affirm the necessity of evangelism, the Reformed theology of that time did not. It adhered to a conception of the State Church, where the gospel was readily made available by compulsive Church attendance, and from there, people were either reprobate or elect, regardless of their will or action. Of course, that point of view ignores people outside Christendom.

## George Fox: The Return of Charisma

While protestant denominations were expunging most traces of the supernatural from their Church life, George Fox had a hard time reconciling the ministries of Christ and the apostles with what he observed in the State Church. He and the first generation of Quakers would practice divine healing, prophetic revelation, and even the casting out of demons.[134]

---

133 Olson, *Story of Christian Theology*, 466, 469.
134 Roberts Liardon, *God's Generals: The Roaring Reformers* (New Kensington, PA: Whitaker House, 2003), 335.

George Fox came to a number of revelations, or "openings" as he called them, about scriptural truths while he endured a few years of theological and philosophical crisis during his youth. His first four major revelations were (1) the reality of the New Birth, (2) the fact that ministerial authority came from the Holy Spirit, not schools, (3) church buildings were not intrinsically holy, and (4) the Holy Spirit was the illuminator of scripture. Though these are common to Christians today, they were heretical to his contemporaries.

Fox and his followers began to evangelize and confront Christians of various denominations with the above revelations. Among other things, Quakers began to draw focus toward the New Birth, and away from concepts of ceremonially derived power.[135] Though it was highly unpopular, they attacked the authority of unconverted ministers. They fought vehemently to point people toward a New Birth experience and leadership from the Holy Spirit rather than from a set of doctrines.

Fox and the Quakers went further. Their meetings were the first to have charismatic expression in the Reformation. Liardon explains that they "believed in being filled with the Holy Spirit with the evidence of speaking in other tongues," and their spiritual experiences included falling over, quivering, and shouting.[136] The spiritual highs of their meetings did not stay contained but translated into profound power evangelism on a scale unprecedented between the Nicene Church and Azusa Street. Fox was attributed

---

135  I use the phrase ceremonial power to describe concepts that Christian virtue, grace, and anointing were conferred through sacraments or other ceremonies. Among these were baptismal regeneration and special power conferred through ordination.

136  Liardon, *God's Generals: The Roaring Reformers*, 357.

with many miraculous healings, including the recovery of stroke victims and the healing of arthritis and lameness.

Fox was also involved in casting out demons. Liardon reports one case of a demonized woman who almost murdered her husband. When Fox came, he confronted the demons, and the woman was delivered.[137] According to what records we have, this was a common occurrence and resulted in the healing of many others with issues of insanity; further, it was not confined to Fox, but like other spiritual experiences, was common among his followers.[138]

Despite the incredible growth of the Quakers during Fox's lifetime, it was not to last. The Church was confronted with a revival that could have restored exorcism, healing, and spiritual gifts three centuries before Azusa Street. What might have happened if it had been accepted? The movement began to flicker out when George Fox died. Fox left his inheritance for the publication of his *Journal* and *Book of Miracles*; however, second-generation Quakers worked quickly to remove healing and exorcism from their Church life and redacted portions of Fox's writing that spoke on healing and exorcism. They destroyed his *Book of Miracles*, severely hampering the continuity of deliverance ministry.

These Quakers were attempting to limit the persecution they received by tuning down their Christianity. It did not work. Unfortunately, Quakers would lean more on prophetic revelation (which was not redacted) and less on the Bible. Today, many Quakers do not even resemble Christians. The rejection of exorcism and healing by English Christians in the seventeenth century was a major mis-

---

137 Liardon, 357.
138 "Records," namely from Fox's *Journal*, Henry Cadbury's reconstruction of *George Fox's "Book of Miracles,"* and David Hodges's *George Fox and the Healing Ministry*.

step of the Church and kept deliverance away for another generation. The self-censoring of second-generation Quakers prevented
anyone from picking up the fight where Fox left off.

## Cotton Mather and New England Puritans

The narrative surrounding the Salem witchcraft debacle is typically
boiled down to wide-eyed religious fanatics hunting down and
killing independently minded women in a gruesome perversion
of justice. Though the witch trials do, in many ways, earn their
reputation as a "witch hunt," the story is not as cut and dry as it is
often taught in public school. In this section, I will primarily examine the point of view of Cotton Mather, a Puritan theologian and
contemporary of the trails. His point of view is important beyond
the witchcraft debacle because he himself was involved in exorcism
as well and had a rather detailed theology on dealing with demons.

### Witchcraft and New England Puritans

Let me preface this section by saying I am not defending the Salem
witch trials or attempting to justify any injustice done there within.
However, as it pertains to this study, I would like to bring to light
some facts about them and the situation in seventeenth-century New
England that critics of the Puritan judicial system typically overlook.

Firstly, many persons condemned for witchcraft in New
England considered themselves witches and attempted to wield
(real or imaginary) malignant powers to manipulate their neighbors. For example, Amy Duny cursed her neighbor's ten-year-old
daughter, saying she would die, and the daughter died three days
later. When the accused appeared in court, she would steadfastly
refuse to repeat the name of Jesus on request. Further, the children

with whom she had contact would enter fits when she was in the room and began coughing up "Crooked Pins; & one time, a Two-penny Nail, with a very broad Head." Another woman cursed by Duny was found paralyzed from the waist down, and a third came down with chronic vomiting. In another case, the same woman cursed a man's horses for damaging her house, saying they would die shortly, and sure enough, they all died within a few days. When the jury convicted Duny, those with lameness and vomiting began to recover.[139]

In another trial, Mather records an incredible story from one witness testifying against Bridget Bishop:

> John Louder Testify'd, that upon some little controversy with Bishop about her fowls, that he did awake in the Night by moonlight, and did see clearly the likeness of this woman grievously oppressing him; in which miserable condition she held him unable to help himself near Day. He told Bishop this; but she deny'd it, and threatened him very much. Quickly after this, being at home on a Lords Day, with the shoors shutt about him, he saw a Black Pig approach him; at which he was going to kick, it vanished away. Immediately after, sitting down, he saw a Black thing Jump in at the Window, & come & stand before him. The Body, was like that of a Monkey, the Feet like a Cocks; but the Face was like a mans. He was being so extremely affrighted, that he

---

139 Cotton Mather, *Wonders of the Invisible World. Observations as Well Historical as Theological, upon the Nature, the Number and the Operations of the Devils (1692)*, ed. Reiner Smolinksi (University of Nebraska-Lincoln), 64–68.

could not speak; this monster spoke to him and said, "I am a Messenger sent unto you, for I understand that you are in some Trouble of Mind, and if you will be ruled by me, you shall want for nothing in thus world.... you had better take my Counsel!" He then struck at it with a stick, but only struck the Ground-sel, and broke the stick. The Arm with which he struck was presently disabled, and it vanished away. He presently went out the back door, and Spyed, this Bishop, in her Orchard, going toward her House; but he had not power to set one foot forward unto her. Whereupon returning to the House, he was immediately accosted by the Monster he had seen before; which Goblin was now going to Fly at him: whereat he cry'd out, "The Whole Armor of God, be between me and you!" so it sprang back, and flew over the Apple-Tree; shaking many Apples off the Tree, in its flying over. At its Leap, it flung dirt with its Feet, against the Stomach of the man; whereon he was then struck Dumb, and so continued for three Days together. Upon the producing of this Testimony, Bishop deny'd that she knew this Despondent: yet their two Orchards and joined, and they had often had their little Quarrels for some years together.[140]

This same Bishop told another one of her neighbors that she was a witch and threatened to curse him if his family didn't do certain labor for her. Another two men who worked on her house found a

---

140 Mather, 82–83.

collection of "puppets" that resembled dolls. She admitted to having these but did not give a reasonable account of their purpose.[141]

A third example cited by Mather was Susan Martin, who cursed a man's cow, which died shortly after. Several people fell ill after receiving Martin's threats. In another case, Martin curses a yoke of Oxen whose owner refused to lend them to her. When they were released to graze, they entered into a frenzy and plunged into the Merrimack River.[142]

Other examples include persons who confessed openly to witchcraft; some refusing to repent, others repenting. All the confessing witches explained they had signed a little book that a demonic figure or another witch presented to them. Many others claimed to have been dragged out of their beds at night by apparitions or demons and offered a chance to sign a book, and when refused, were beaten.[143] Perhaps the most chilling example is that of a witch tried several decades before the Salem ordeal, who was tried for both murder and witchcraft. The accused confessed openly to a plot of witchcraft, boldly claiming that they would extinguish Christianity from New England.[144]

The reader is not obligated to believe the accounts presented by Mather. However, as mentioned previously, what is important when examining history is not whether supernatural occurrences can or did take place but whether the people at that time and place believed they did. The reality is that the Puritans believed that underground witchcraft was spreading and causing real, supernat-

---

141 Mather, 84.
142 Mather, 86–88.
143 Mather, 86–88.
144 Mather, xii.

ural evil in New England. Further, many of the people accused of witchcraft did believe themselves to be witches and that they could wield satanic power.

## Cotton Mather and Exorcism

In 1689 and 1692, Mather published two works detailing his theology of spiritual warfare: *Memorable Providences* and *Wonders of the Invisible World*. In both, Mather counsels his readers to combat demons and witches with spiritual means rather than civil. Prosecution of witchcraft should be the last order of business, and only when ample evidence had been provided to prove the case. He implores all the Christians of New England to repent of accusations and gossip and to join in the unity of faith in prayer and fasting. He points out that even those accused of witchcraft needed to be delivered and that love should be extended to them. He counsels those accused of witchcraft to fast, pray, and repent in order to see deliverance.[145]

In *Providences*, Mather gives several accounts of possessed persons in Boston and the accounts of their deliverance, which involved prolonged periods of fasting and prayer by Mather and other pastors in the area. In these prayer sessions, Mather did several experiments; he presented a variety of books before the victim and observed more violent demonic reactions than those that Mather considered theologically orthodox and none with novels or heretical literature. He would have a Bible opened somewhere the victim could not see or hear; still, there was an immediate demonic reaction.[146]

---

145 Mather, xxx.
146 Cotton Mather, *Memorable Providences* (Gale Ecco, Sabin Americana), 8–30.

Mather's narrative was followed by two sermons in which he preached demonology and spiritual warfare. In them, Mather clearly explained that even converted Christians could be demonized. He warned of all kinds of doors that could lead to this. "Every lust, as it were, surrenders us up unto the devil. Every time a man gratified a lust, a devil is invited into the soul of that man, and by every new act of it, he takes hold of the soul." And further, "The Devil finds a place in the soul of [an angry man]... discontentment opens the doors of the soul for all the devils of hell to enter it."[147]

Mather also addresses issues with suicide, which he believed were from demonic spirits. His counsel to those struggling was to seek out help and talk to someone. He explained that the stronghold of chronic suicide ideations was often the result of some "old and great sin, unrepented of," and that carefully searching for whatever that door was, and closing it, would bring deliverance.[148]

Mather also described a case of a *Christian* who became possessed. When the demon was asked how it entered, it said that it found grounds to dwell on. He warns his audience that any of them are susceptible to demonization if they are not walking in holiness and vigilant in prayer. He said, "The father of lies uttered an awful truth, when he said through the mouth of a possessed man, 'if God would give me leave, I would find enough [sin] in the best of you all, to make you all mine.'"[149]

*Wonders* is opened with doctrinal statements about the Devil and demons. The first is that no one doubts the existence of Satan unless they themselves are demonized. There are also countless

---

147  Mather, 61.
148  Mather, 65–66.
149  Mather, 78–80.

demons, and sometimes thousands of them can demonize one person. The Devil and demons are also the root source of all temptation. Further, there is a "military government" in Satan's kingdom, and that some demons are more qualified to afflict certain regions. It is further explained that the satanic kingdom is allowed by God to afflict man; this allowance of this affliction is according to "Law," which opens humanity to attack. The ultimate goal of these attacks is bodily possession. The Devil also drives national evils, witchcraft, plagues, and various types of destruction.[150]

There are also diverse types of demons, "an unclean spirit, a drinking spirit, a swearing spirit, a worldly spirit, a passionate spirit, a revengeful spirit." There is no amount of holiness that made Christians immune from demons, as Mather points out that even David was influenced by Satan to take a census. Beyond our own personal sins, Mather explains that the sins of past generations are held to accord in the current generation and that as each generation goes by, "men will become more... refined in the arts of sinning."[151]

In short, casting out demons was part of the experience of Mather and his area of influence. He seems to have a system of various degrees of demonization, using terms like possessed, oppressed, and vexed. Regardless of the description, in each case, the solution seems to be prolonged times of fasting and prayer until there is definite recovery of the victims. Several instances cited by Mather were Christians demonized as a result of "bewitchment." Many of the symptoms have already been named, including the immediate development of chronic illness, fits of violence and screaming, and

---

150 Mather, *Wonders of the Invisible World*, 4–11.
151 Mather, 15–18.

other strange episodes.[152] Most of the people bewitched in *Wonders* were otherwise "particularly noted for goodness and virtue."[153]

The method of deliverance Mather prescribes for these demonized people is first confession, repentance, prayer, and fasting. Mather also employed highly forensic elements in exorcism, including detailed observation and interrogation. Most importantly, victims must search and find the root cause of sin and close the door through repentance.

The activity of spiritual warfare was not limited to demons afflicting people but to territorial spirits binding the land as "principalities and powers." Neither is it limited to ministers or specially called persons. According to Mather, spiritual warfare was the obligation of every Christian in New England, regardless of age, position, or denomination. All are to pray "Incessant and Vehement prayers," which Mather says are "that great Artillery of Heaven." He says that even the "most obscure Christian" can have the most effective prayers against the Devil and toward the deliverance of persons, and of the land itself.[154]

In conclusion, Mather taught that the physical world was controlled by an invisible, spiritual conflict, ultimately governed by God. According to the degrees of God's law, at times, Satan is allowed to afflict mankind, bind regions in unbelief and demonism, and possess persons, even at times virtuous Christians. The situation in New England resulted from backslidings in the Christian Church, and the solution was repentance and a consistent, aggressive campaign of prayer and fasting. Witches and witchcraft play a

---

152 Mather, 60–90.
153 Mather, 52.
154 Mather, 56.

role in this war, but they are not the true enemy, merely the fruit of spiritual sickness, and Christians need to keep their crosshairs on the enemy in prayer and not be preoccupied with witch hunts.

## Conclusions

Exorcism and spiritual warfare were not common among early protestants. Early protestants' rigid theological systems became their dominant feature, despite moves toward "heart religion" by some groups. These systematic theologians would continue to harden against the continuation of miracles, mostly as a reaction to Catholic claims of the supernatural.

As noted above, the three notable exceptions to the lack of exorcism for early protestants were the early Lutheran exorcism, the charismatic ministry of Fox and Quakers, and the ministry of Cotton Mather. These three approaches mirror the ritual, charismatic, and forensic approaches to exorcism, respectively.

For Lutherans, baptismal exorcism did have real spiritual power to deliver the baptismal recipient from generational and original sin. Many thought of the rite as having tremendous importance in guarding children from demonic influence. As we have seen, the significance of this rite decreased over time until it was eliminated. This rite, being a part of a sacrament, could, of course, only be administered by an ordained minister in the Lutheran Church. The question about Christians and demonization was not important. In the "Church-State," all citizens were Christians, and so any demonization that did take place (and it did) would have been demonized Christians.

For Quakers, casting out demons was not a rite but a charismatic action of the Spirit of God through a faith-filled vessel. It was used to cure insanities and certain sicknesses, and other forms of demonism. In this style, exorcism was not limited to any minister or specially gifted person but any Christian who exercised faith. As far as I've found, Fox and first-generation Quakers didn't define whether Christians could be demonized; it is possible they did not because they adhered to a form of Christian perfectionism.

For Mather-Puritans, exorcism was neither a rite nor a charismatic action but a forensic process that involved time and energy in prayer and fasting and sought to remedy the root cause of a problem. Mather-Puritans would use exorcism to remedy demonization where it was present and in various forms, which included madness and sickness. This demonism was sometimes the result of witchcraft, but not always, and often entirely unrelated. Spiritual warfare and exorcism were the responsibility of all Christians and should be engaged in corporately when possible. Finally, Mather was very clear about Christians being demonized, even those who were especially virtuous.

The above three examples represent a minority at this time. Why did most other Christians ignore spiritual warfare? Reformed theology was an increasingly influential factor in the West, and it was a strong reaction against Catholic theology in almost every way. The Catholic Church continued to espouse exorcism and various healing miracles, and Reformed theology reacted by denying them, at first in practice and later in systematic theology.

It can be questioned what benefit these three views of spiritual warfare brought to the Church. I cannot point to any evidence other than my conjecture or opinion. But if these ministries were null, why did they experience so much opposition? All three of these forms of spiritual warfare were highly resisted and redacted from history, preventing a continuity of exorcism from one generation to the other. The Reformed Church was given the opportunity to have the full gospel restored in the same power as the early Church; however, they stopped short at the doctrine of justification. The chance to restore the full gospel would return again in the next generation at the Great Awakening.

CHAPTER 7

# REASON AND REVIVALISM:
## THE BIRTH OF EVANGELICALISM
### AD 1700-1900

## The Effects of the Enlightenment on Protestantism

As the Enlightenment swept the Western world, it drastically changed much of Christian theology. Beliefs in the supernatural, a spiritual world, and miracles were challenged by the scientific revolution. The Catholic Church resisted its influence to a degree and maintained its traditional understanding of spiritual matters, though it may have been less emphasized. Protestants, who were not predisposed to the supernatural anyway, embraced some aspects of the Enlightenment by developing the doctrine of cessationism.

Calvin was the first to espouse cessationism, as a way to explain the apparent lack of miracles, contrast to what was read in Acts, and to discredit the reported supernatural activity of the Catholic Church. However, this point of view was not mainstream among first-generation protestants. Cessationism rose to greater popularity along with anti-Catholic sentiments in the 1700s and 1800s. A disdain for "popish" magic tricks and an increasing attraction to science and reason drove protestants away from miracles.[155]

Cessationism was not the only theological reaction to the Enlightenment. A much stronger embrace of reason came in the form of Deism. Deists not only rejected most or all contemporary miracles but cleared Christianity of any of its "backward" and unscientific thinking. The morality of the Bible and its authority as God's word are in most cases affirmed. But the miracles of Jesus and supernatural events of the Bible were interpreted as fictional, or seriously doubted. The simplest and most common summary of Deism is that God created the universe and set moral laws in place but does not at all intervene in the course of history.

Though Deism was relatively short-lived, its influence along with cessationism made eighteenth- and nineteenth-century protestantism a hostile environment for divine healing, exorcism, and other charismatic expressions. Lutheran exorcism, Quaker revivalism, and the spiritual warfare theology of Mather were firmly expunged from their own areas of influence.

## The Advent of Evangelicalism

The theology of Arminius and the practices of the Moravians would combine nicely into the person and ministry of John Wesley to create the headwaters of evangelical Christianity. The concept of a Church-State was being challenged for some time

---

155 Thomas Kidd, "The Healing of Mercy Wheeler: Illness and Miracles among Early American Evangelicals," *William and Mary Quarterly* 63, no. 1 (January 2006): 164.

in England by Puritans, who maintained that not every baptized citizen was truly converted, and therefore, not really part of the Church. That sentiment was similar for Methodists, but rather than seeking to purify the Church of the unconverted, they sought to evangelize them and emphasis methods of holy living. At first, this evangelism was confined to the Church building, but, with the encouragement of George Whitefield, and resistance of Anglican leadership, Wesley moved outdoors and began street preaching.

The creation of evangelicalism is significant for this study because it represents a step toward a recovery of the New Testament program. The first generation of reformers recovered some scriptural truths and biblical principles but did not recover the practices and actions that should have corresponded with these principles. As previously mentioned, until the Moravians, evangelism, or missions of any kind from protestants, didn't exist.

Wesley and the Methodists sought to restore principles of evangelism and discipleship, not just in foreign missions, but in their own neighborhood. The necessity of evangelism, which is probably a given to most readers, was a novel concept. Without it, the development of healing and exorcism would have likely been as stunted as they were before.

## The Replacement of the State Church

One of the key steps in the development of evangelical Christianity was the decline of the State Church. Shelley points out that "thirty generations" of Christianity went by with the harmonious balance of the Church preparing lay people for heaven and the State maintaining Christian society. With the Reformation,

Church unity was brought to an end.[156] In the American colonies, there was no State Church. Without compulsion from the law, the Church needed to convince people of its veracity and evangelize the lost, through revival.[157]

The First and Second Great Awakening represent the apex of the early forms of revival. In both Awakenings and the smaller revivals that took place in between, thousands of people would gather to hear a great evangelist. In a large crowd, emotions and the power of God would run high, resulting in massive groups of people repenting and being converted. At times, there were "fainting" spells; some would go into fits, similar to some of the manifestations that happened with the early Quakers. Typically, these manifestations were either ignored or condemned by the preacher, but they happened nonetheless.

Regardless of whatever did happen, the goal of the evangelists was met; people had dramatic born-again experiences, Church attendance skyrocketed, and the Christianity of America was firmly maintained.

### Evangelicalism and Miracles

Despite the anti-miracle environment of protestantism, the new wave and evangelicalism did experience some notable movements of the supernatural. Kidd records some involuntary manifestations of the supernatural that took place during the First Great Awakening, including "trances, fits, and even instant healings." Cessational revivalists struggled with how to qualify these happenings, as they

---

156 Shelley, *Church History in Plain Language*, 358.
157 Shelley, 359.

were not the result of a preacher's instigation. So they did come with limited acceptance.[158]

One well-documented case that couldn't be explained away was the miraculous healing of Mercy Wheeler. Wheeler was lame from childhood and came to believe the Lord would heal her at a certain revival meeting. Sure enough, after that revival meeting, she recovered the ability to walk.[159] Other healings and miracles also took place during the First Great Awakening, though Kidd points out that proponents of the revival carefully avoided the word "miracle" and attempted to maintain a distance from too much interest in the supernatural.

While much of the evangelical movement took place within previously established denominations, the Methodists were the first purely evangelical organization. The ministry of John Wesley and first-generation Methodists were a more tolerant place for the supernatural. Methodism set itself apart with a focus on evangelism, discipleship, spiritual disciplines, and holiness. Nothing about these main traits directly related to the supernatural. However, as Methodists were more intentional about their fervor toward God, it's understandable why more outbreaks of the supernatural occurred with them. Roberts Liardon recounts that large Methodist prayer meetings were emotionally charged, high energy, and long lasting. He cites examples of people being struck to the ground in conviction and repentance.

John Wesley had several notable cases of exorcisms. At many of these high-charged meetings, demons would begin to manifest in people. Liardon cites the following example of an "upstanding

158 Kidd, "The Healing of Mercy Wheeler," 164.
159 Kidd, 164.

churchman" who entered a demonic fit after being exposed to a sermon on salvation:

> After he read the last line, his face changed color and he fell from his chair, screaming and beating himself against the ground. The Wesley brothers were called, and they came and quickly as possible. When they arrived, they found the house full of people; Hayden [the victim] was in the same unusual state. Hayden's wife had first tried to keep everyone out, but Hayden cried out, "No; let them come; let all the world see the just judgment of God." As John entered, he announced to those present, "Ay, this is he who, I said, was a deceiver of the people. But God has overtaken me. I said it was a delusion; but this is no delusion." Then he roared, "O thou devil! Thou cursed devil! Yea, thou legion of devils! Thou canst stay. Christ will cast thee out! I know His work is begun. Tear me to pieces, if thou wilt; but thou canst not hurt me." As soon as he had spoken, he began beating himself on the ground again, his chest heaving and sweat rolling off his face. The Wesley brothers and those with them began to pray earnestly, continuing until the seizures had stopped.[160]

In another instance, a Christian woman was manifesting very violently for several days straight. Both the Wesleys and some others prayed for the woman for a long period of time. When Charles

---

160 Roberts Liardon, *God's Generals: The Revivalists* (New Kensington, PA: Whitaker House, 2008), 61.

Wesley entered the house, the demon screamed, "Preacher! Field preacher! I don't love field-preaching." The battle began to break when one person present engaged in a combative dialogue with the demons, wearing them down. Finally, the woman was delivered. Other instances of healings and exorcisms were fairly common in John's ministry.[161]

When examining these frequent "fits" and other emotional displays during this revival, Liardon points out that the vocabulary, understanding, and Church culture were entirely different than they are for us today. Words like "demonic manifestation" and "slain in the spirit" were not in use. Words like "deliverance" or "exorcism" would have meant something entirely different at that time. Further, these happenings were not precedented. They are common among Pentecostals and charismatics today, and most evangelicals are moderately familiar with these experiences and their related vocabulary. If someone fell into what I would define as a "demonic manifestation," the people of this time would not have had the experience, knowledge, or vocabulary to describe what was happening in a way the modern reader can accurately understand it.[162]

In their respective interviews with me, Roberts Liardon and Bob Larson both made mention of these fits, and they alluded to the possibility that many of these were demonic manifestations that were misunderstood and unaddressed. According to this theory, anointed preachers like Whitefield and other revivalists would preach the gospel, and the Holy Spirit would move in the massive audiences. People among those listening were probably demonized (without knowing it) and their afflicting spirits reacted violently.

161  Liardon, 62–65.
162  Roberts Liardon, interview.

Despite these reactions, ministers typically wouldn't respond by expelling these spirits.[163]

The profound experiences, and their commonality to Wesley's ministry, and other manifestations that took place during the Awakening were not to last. Like the exorcism and healing of Quakerism and baptismal exorcism, the strong criticism of "Old Lights"[164] was able to successfully wipe out the move toward restoration of the charismatic gifts. Roberts Liardon points out that Jonathan Edwards, who was respected by both the Old Lights and the revivalists, defended many aspects of the Awakening. However, he condemned "tongues, prophecy, healing and working of miracles" as "delusions." By Liardon's estimation, had Edwards and some of his contemporaries accepted these manifestations, America could have been founded as a "charismatic Christian nation that operated in the power of the first-century church."[165]

## Blumhardt's Battle

While the revivals were taking place in the English-speaking world, a Lutheran pastor of a small town in Germany would have a notable account of spiritual warfare.

A young woman from an impoverished family began to experience a "haunting" at her residence, and eventually she began to manifest demons. Pastor Blumhardt, after initially rejecting the phenomena, began to confront and expel the spirits. As the spirits were confronted, the victim would have unusual manifestations, such has vomiting "buckets" of water and displaying other unex-

---

163  Bob Larson, interview.
164  "Old Lights" refers to ministers who opposed the Awakening and emotionalism.
165  Liardon, God's Generals: The Revivalists, 166.

plainable medical issues. Later in the course of the battle, the victim began to expel nails, pins, and broken glass from her mouth, nose, and other parts of the body. At times, Blumhardt even claimed to have witnessed live animals emerge from the victim's throat.[166] After two years of persistent exorcism, prayer, and fasting, the victim was finally delivered and would go on to become well known for virtue and charity.

Blumhardt's belief was that this exorcism weakened the forces of darkness over the entire region, and it was what led to the subsequent revival and numerous healing miracles that would later accompany his ministry. Notably, the severely demonized woman was described as a Christian of legitimate conversion before her exorcism, according to Blumbardt's estimation. He attributed this severe demonization to the works of black magicians who unsuccessfully tried to recruit the girl.

The long-term effects of this exorcism and the micro-revival that followed are difficult to discern as Germany was swallowed by liberal theology in the late nineteenth century, snuffing out any continuity.

## Conclusions

The eighteenth and nineteenth centuries were a relative lull in exorcism, when compared with the Reformation and the following revival of Pentecostalism. However, during periods of revival, there were sporadic occasions of exorcism, and perhaps more demonic manifestations that were not dealt with. In those times when demons were expelled, such as the notable examples of Blumhardt and Wesley, they

---

166 Johann Christoph Blumhardt, *Jesus Is Victor!: Blumhardt's Battle with the Powers of Darkness* (Ebersbach an der Fils, Germany: AwakenMedia, 2020).

were both ministers. At a time when exorcism was a faint memory of previous generations, that had an air of mystery and supernaturalism, the only person to call for help would be a local pastor, and hope that he had the wherewithal to deal with the situation.

By and large, the theologies of the eighteenth and nineteenth centuries were not supportive of exorcism or other supernatural expressions. Though Methodists initially accepted the supernatural, most English-speaking protestants embraced cessationism. Later generations of Methodists would become more akin to the other protestants, de-emphasizing the supernatural.

## Revival and Reason: Effects on Exorcism

As the nineteenth century progressed, liberal theology appeared in Germany and rapidly swept the Western world, influencing much of Christianity. Revival, the supernatural, took a back seat; the very authority of the scripture was at stake, in a world that revolved around scientism and natural observation. Other secular influences contributed to this battle, which backed Christianity into a corner and slowly expunged it from secular parts of society. As Christianity struggled to prove its reasonableness, exorcism and other charismatic expressions became dangerous liabilities, not worth being carried. Even Catholicism distanced itself from spiritual warfare in the nineteenth century.

While this battle took place, the doctrine that Christians could not be demonized began to cement in a stronger way. Though it had been held by some since the time of Calvin, during the nineteenth century, it became mainstream. As cessationism explained the lack of miracles, the non-demonization of Christians explained the lack of exorcism, and its lack of need.

In those precious few places where demons were expelled during this period, it was considered a crucial part of revival. Demons were fought viciously over periods of time, and these exorcisms were largely forensic, employing interrogation of the demons and looking for causes and solutions to the problem.

## Deliverance Redacted from Revival

This was a period that started with some of the most powerful and influential revivals since the time of the early Church. The Lord restored the necessity of evangelism in the infant nation of America, and this would trigger the missionary movement of the nineteenth century; these two centuries represented the most forward progress of the great commission since the second century. However, these incredible forward movements were handicapped. Deliverance from the demonic was rejected or ignored; it allowed for infiltration and hampering of revival and slowed the missional work in heathen nations until Pentecostal exorcism arrived in the twentieth century, which sped it forward.

We can only wonder what kind of world we would be living in if Edwards and his colleagues had the revelation of the Baptism of the Holy Spirit and the charismatic gifts that they rejected. If Liardon is correct, we could have had Pentecostal restoration two centuries earlier. Who knows what kind of good could have been accomplished? What if the others had embraced deliverance from the demonic that Wesley practiced? Exorcism, tongues, and healing were redacted from these revivals, waiting another century before their potential restoration.

CHAPTER 8

# PENTECOSTALISM:
## UNCHECKED SPIRITUAL POWER
### AD 1880-1950

## Proto-Pentecostalism

The Azusa Street Revival of 1906 was the genesis of the Pentecostal movement. However, several people and revivals exhibited aspects that would grow into Pentecostalism later. By the turn of the century, exorcism was not at all common in American or Western Christianity, outside some possible, rare occurrences in liturgical denominations. The Pentecostal movement and its antecedents brought a renewal of perspective to exorcism, at least initially, due to its focus on the supernatural. For this section, we will review the ministries of John Alexander Dowie and Maria Woodworth-Etter, as two revivalists who brought new attention to the supernatural. Shortly after the turn of the century, the Welsh Revival proved to be another source of inspiration to Azusa Street and produced an interesting understanding of spiritual warfare in its own right.

## John Alexander Dowie

Unlike many names reviewed in this study, Dowie did not have much focus on expelling demons or spiritual warfare, and his significance is mostly in his influence upon the Pentecostal movement. He began his ministry as a pastor in Australia; his proto-Pentecostalism began when he was chronically confronted with sickness in his Church and sought a solution, coming to divine healing. Liardon quotes the following from Dowie:

> Where, oh where, was He Who used to heal His suffering children? No prayer for healing seemed to reach His ear, and yet I knew His hand had not been shortened . . . It seemed sometimes as if I could almost hear the triumphant mockery of fiends ringing in my ear whilst I spoke to the bereaved ones the words of Christian hope and consolation. Disease, the foul offspring of its father, Satan, and its mother, Sin, was defiling and destroying . . . and there was no deliverer . . . Then the words of the Holy Ghost inspired in Acts 10:38, stood before me all radiant with light, revealing Satan as the defiler, and Christ as the Healer.

Shortly after this revelation, Dowie was called to minister to a dying Christian. Though this was common in his ministry up until this point, this time he prayed a prayer of faith, and the person was healed. According to Liardon, from that revelation onward, no members of Dowie's Church died of disease.[167]

---

167 Roberts Liardon, *God's Generals: Why They Succeeded and Why Some Failed* (New Kensington, PA: Whitaker House, 1996), 25–26.

Eventually, Dowie left his pastoral ministry, trundled through a brief political career, and then into itinerate ministry in the United States. His popularity grew, and with it, so did his ego. Since he was apparently the only evangelist operating in divine healing, he concluded that he was the end times Elijah, and founded Zion, a city in the Midwest dedicated to his loose religious following. This city would eventually be the meeting place of several influential Pentecostal leaders in the next generation.

Dowie was apparently not involved in any sort of exorcism, but if he was, it didn't impact the Church at large. Further, he was opposed to tongues and the Baptism of the Holy Spirit. However, his reintroduction of divine healing proved influential to later Pentecostals who would come out of Azusa Street.

## Maria Woodworth-Etter

Meanwhile, another prominent evangelist arose who brought significant media attention to the supernatural: Maria Woodworth-Etter. Like Dowie, Etter was also extremely controversial, but not because of personality scandals as much as the fact she was a female preacher in the nineteenth century. The manifestations that would eventually be a hallmark of her meetings, while perhaps at home among contemporary Pentecostals, were considered quite bizarre for her day. While Dowie pioneered a divine healing ministry, Etter expanded into other areas we would normally consider Pentecostal, such as trances, tongues, and revelatory gifts. Because there was a terrible disdain in denomination circles surrounding healing, Etter initially stayed clear of it and other theological debacles, believing she was called as purely an evangelist and that the supernatural had nothing to do with that.

After praying and studying the scriptures, Etter came to the conclusion that healing *was* part of an evangelistic calling. Liardon describes her epiphany as follows: "She studied the word and began to preach [God's] divine will to heal. It didn't take long to see evangelism and healing went hand in hand, as thousands were won to Christ as the result of seeing others healed. Maria preached [healing was] 'nothing new... just something the church had lost.'"[168] As healing became a part of her ministry, her publicity increased greatly due to the draw of miracles, and other supernatural occurrences began to follow her as well. She was most noted for people falling into trances in the midst of her meetings, something she claims to have done nothing to trigger, and was initially opposed to herself.[169]

Almost immediately after Etter began laying hands on the sick, she began also to cast out demons. For her ministry, and classical Pentecostalism that followed, the line between healing and exorcism was blurry. Hands were laid and a forceful command using the name of Jesus was repeated until the demon or sickness left. Using this method, Etter expelled a deaf and dumb spirit at one of her meetings, which resulted in the healing of the deaf man.[170] With healing and deliverance mixed, and a lack of vocabulary to describe spiritual warfare, many of the accounts are unclear whether Etter was dealing with a demon or a sickness; many times that a demon was "rebuked" or we see other elements reminiscent of spiritual warfare, they were used against a physical illness, which

---

168  Roberts Liardon, *God's Generals: Why They Succeeded and Why Some Fail* (New Kensington, PA: Whitaker House, 1996), 55.
169  Liardon, 52.
170  Liardon, 64.

was thought to be either directly caused by a demon or the indirect result of demonic influence in the natural world.

Etter also reintroduced the practice of spiritual warfare with principalities. One example of this was when Etter attempted to preach in a town known for its resistance to evangelism. After a few days of preaching with no results, Etter began to eviscerate the principalities, praying against all ruling demonic forces and binding them. Shortly after this, people began to repent. Etter taught and used similar tactics in later meetings, something that impacted later Pentecostal leaders who saw it.

## The Welsh Revival

The Welsh Revival was the immediate inspiration of Seymour and the Azusa Street Mission. Unlike Azusa Street, it did not produce any major theological or practical shift in the Church; however, it left a lasting, positive impact on the nation of Wales, which was entirely "turned over" for several years during the revival.

The revival ended when Evan Roberts collapsed from exhaustion and was spirited away to England by Jessie Penn-Lewis. The validity of this course of action is debated. Dr. Liardon and most Pentecostals consider this a jezebelian abduction; others believe that this saved Robert's life. The result was the slow death of the revival and a litany of literature produced by Roberts and Penn-Lewis during his time in England.

Most significantly for this study was *War on the Saints* in which Penn-Lewis makes the case that passivity and unguarded acceptance of the supernatural in the Church was a leading cause of demonization among Christians, and that a lack of wisdom, discernment, and deliverance was leading to a mass demonic infiltration into the

Church. This unchecked demonization was the leading cause of the collapse of revivals, the slowdown of evangelism, and the proliferation of liberal theology. Despite being largely ignored by classical Pentecostals, *War on the Saints* however was an early attempt to bring awareness to the demonization in the Church, and it would later influence the deliverance ministries of the preceeding generation.

## Azusa Street: The Divorce of Deliverance

What set Pentecostalism firmly apart from its predecessors and other denominations was its strong emphasis on the Baptism of the Holy Spirit with the evidence of speaking in tongues. This experience was common to the apostolic Church, and it remained present in some monastic settings throughout the early Middle Ages. In the mainline Church, it slowly evolved into the Catholic rite of "confirmation." After the Reformation, protestants did not make any delineation between conversion and the reception of the Holy Spirit, and so the concept fell by the wayside. As the revivalists of the eighteenth and nineteenth centuries read the scripture, they saw this experience, subsequent to conversion, and began to seek this second blessing, as though groping in the dark.

The Pentecostal understanding of baptism began at a school in Topeka, Kansas, with Charles Parham. Parham assigned his students to research the Baptism of the Holy Spirit from the scripture, and to report their findings. They found that it was an empowering experience that was evidenced by speaking in tongues. The students and staff began to pray for this baptism, and they soon began to experience ecstatic, spiritual manifestations, followed by speaking in tongues. News of these events spread rapidly, and people came to see what these occurrences were about.

Among those interested in these spiritual experiences was an African American named William Seymour. Seymour listened to Parham's lectures at school from outside the class window, limited by contemporary segregation laws, and he was inspired by the message about the Baptism of the Holy Spirit. As he prayed for revival, he received a letter from a Church in Los Angeles, inviting him to preach; when he preached on the Baptism of the Holy Spirit, he was locked out and found refuge with a local family who was also praying for revival. He and the family prayed and began to have similar dramatic spiritual experiences; when news spread, they were joined by others, and soon the house was overflowing with people, forcing Seymour to rent a large barn on Azusa Street, marking the beginning of the historic revival in 1906.

The revival drew worldwide attention, with ministers and laity visiting from far and wide. Tommy Welchel's *They Told Me Their Stories* recounts an oral history of some of those who regularly attended the revival. He records that incredible healings took place, including the growing of an amputee's leg.[171] The attendees also reported a cloud often overtaking the room, like a fog, which was believed to be the Glory of God.[172] At several points, neighbors called the fire department, reporting a massive conflagration on the roof of the building; when the fire department would arrive, there would be no fire, and this too was attributed to the Glory of God.[173]

The revival produced classical Pentecostal revivalists such as John G. Lake and F. F. Bosworth. These revivalists, and many

---

171 Tommy Welchel, J. Edward Morris, and Cindy McCowan, *Azusa Street: They Told Me Their Stories: The Youth and Children of Azusa Street Tell Their Stories* (Mustang, Oklahoma: Dare2Dream Books, 2006), 77.

172 Welchel, Morris, and McCowan, 91.

173 Welchel, Morris, and McCowan, 37.

others, brought their experiences back to their hometowns. Some felt that their tongues correlated to the language of a specific nation and felt led to go to these nations on missions. Pentecostalism spread rapidly, especially in America and later Africa.

Over the course of the first year, the revival began to get out of control, and Seymour worried that it was developing spiritualistic and unbiblical elements. He began to write letters to Parham begging him to come and help him discern what was true and false, and to bring order to the meeting.[174] By the time Parham did arrive, he described the revival as having the following:

> manifestations of the flesh, spiritualistic controls... people practicing hypnotism at the altar over candidates seeking baptism, though many were receiving the real baptism of the Holy Ghost... I found hypnotic influences, spiritualistic influences, familiar spirit influences, mesmeric influences and all kinds of spells, spasms, falling in trances, etc.[175]

Parham led some meetings at Azusa and attempted to purify the revival by preventing the bizarre manifestations and exorcising those who had been so affected. This, however, was an affront to Seymour, who saw this as an attempt to control the Holy Spirit. He responded by kicking Parham out and padlocking his quarters. Parham then rented a nearby building and held a number of revival meetings, where he exorcised "between two and three hundred who had been possessed of awful fits and spasms and controls in the

174 Liardon, *God's Generals: Why They Succeeded and Why Some Fail*, 126.
175 Liardon, 158.

Azusa Street work."[176] Thus, according to Parham, the Holy Spirit-baptized Christians at Azusa Street fell victim to demonization and needed to be delivered. Parham further understood the Azusa Street Revival to have been infiltrated with demonic influences, and he sought to exorcise those who had been bewitched through the abovementioned practices, and to set up guards to prevent spiritualistic influences from entering the revival again.

Exorcism *was* practiced in the Azusa, before and after Parham's visit; however, it was from an entirely different point of view. The first context was in healing, when there was reason to suspect a sickness was demonic, such as a "deaf and dumb" spirit or a spirit of infirmity. The second was when a manifestation could in no way be attributed to the Holy Spirit and was very clearly demonic. However, most manifestations that most of us would probably consider to be demonic were attributed to the Holy Spirit. So, where exorcism did take place, it was either reactive or in pursuit of healing.

Parham by contrast understood the Baptism of the Holy Spirit in a stricter sense, as an empowering experience that was evidenced by tongues. Other manifestations present at Azusa, such as moans, screams, spasms, and animalism were the works of demons and spiritism. All this sort of nonsense Parham would have cleared out with exorcism and maybe some teaching on the matter. He believed that the revival was a work of God, and that people were actually being baptized in the Holy Spirit. However, baptism was *not* a sure guard against bewitchment and demonization. The freedom left by Seymour allowed demonism to infiltrate and infect the revival, and it evidenced his lack of discernment. By Parham's reading, the bizarre

---

176 Liardon, 158.

manifestations were not only demonic in their own right, but they produced bad fruit.[177] He explained that the bewitched persons were filled with pride and error, "... feel exalted, thinking they have a greater experience than anyone else, not needing instruction or advise... placing them out of reach from those who can help."[178]

Despite Parham's efforts from across the street, the Azusa Street Revival collapsed about a year after his expulsion. A secretary, offended at Seymour's marriage, abducted the mailing list for the newsletter and moved to Oregon. The newsletter was the biggest source of financial support and publicity for the revival, and without it, the revival began to peter out, and reports of the incredible occurrences also ceased.[179]

The decision to divorce deliverance and the manner of thinking that influenced it still affects the Church today. All the major denominations that came from Azusa Street have by and large rejected the ministry of deliverance. Though they have a foggy idea that demons are cast out, sometime, somewhere, it is typically not a part of their ministries. Though previous protestants believed that Christians could not have demons, its theology foundation was cessationism. For classical Pentecostals, the non-demonization of Christians would spring from the centrality of the Baptism of the Holy Spirit to the Christian experience. As Pentecostals had a powerful, definable filling with the Holy Spirit, over time, it was assumed that this powerful experience would be deliverance itself; exorcism was not necessary. After all, how could the Holy Spirit cohabitate with demons?

---

177 Liardon, 128.
178 Liardon, 128.
179 Liardon, 161.

This hyperfocus on the baptism, and the divorce of deliverance from Pentecostalism's inception, would lead to those denominations and cultures that came from this point to by and large reject exorcism.

## Classical Pentecostalism

The missionaries and evangelists that went forth from Azusa Street were by and large rejected by the Churches to which they returned, and they ended up forming their own local assemblies. They attracted primarily the lower classes of society and were made up of the poor and uneducated. The classical Pentecostals of the decades after Azusa held a negative stigma as being poor and uneducated.

Throughout the 1920s and '30s, Pentecostals still met for camp meetings and had periodic revivals, which included healing and sporadic exorcism. However, by the '40s Pentecostalism had begun to organize into denominations, and slowly lost its revivalism. In this environment of spiritual decline resulted the defunct Latter Rain movement. Despite this slow, downward trajectory, several prominent figures maintained ministries that saw incredible healings and some deliverance. We will briefly examine three of them for this study.

### John G. Lake

Though he was most well known for healing, Lake also exorcised demons as no small part of his ministry. Shortly after his time at Azusa, Lake spent six days fasting and praying; in the conclusion, he felt God gave him a special calling to discern and expel demons,[180]

---

180  Liardon, 178.

and from that point on he confronted and expelled demons on a regular basis. Liardon describes a classic example of this: "In the group was a man who fell to the floor in front of the platform in an epileptic seizure. Immediately, Lake jumped off the platform and was at his side, rebuking the demon in the name of Jesus. After the man was restored, Lake quickly returned to the platform."[181] In another account, Lake and his Church in South Africa were interceding for a man in a Welsh insane asylum. During that time of prayer, Lake fell into a trance and saw himself standing before the afflicted man in Wales, laying his hands on and quickly expelling the demon, resulting in the man's restoration.[182]

For Lake, spiritual warfare as a whole encompassed a universal battle against the forces of Satan, who was primarily a thief, a murderer, and a destroyer, his work causing misery, pain, sickness, and death. Casting out demons was only one small front in this battle. Sickness, a much further-reaching extension of Satan's kingdom, was seen as one of the main targets, attacked through divine healing.

Lake's efforts in Africa had an outstanding impact on the history of exorcism. He, along with other Pentecostal missionaries, brought a completely new dynamic to the mission field in Africa. Historian Allan Anderson attributes exorcism to one of the leading factors in the rapid growth of Pentecostalism in Africa, while mainstream protestant missionaries had not produced results because of their disconnection with the African understanding of the spiritual world. The Enlightenment-influenced missionaries tended to denounce tribal African religion as foolishness and falsehood, with-

---

181 Liardon, 180.
182 Liardon, 184.

out answering the fact that native witch doctors had more spiritual power than Christian missionaries.[183]

Lake and other Pentecostal missionaries brought a dynamic that was much more successful among Africans: pagan spiritual experiences were not make believe, but demonic. In similar fashion to the early Church, the missionaries could exorcise the spirits that the Africans were familiar with, forcing them into a combative dialogue. Here the missionaries could publicly prove that the God they preached was more powerful than the native spirits invoked by the Africans. When spiritual warfare became tangible, Africa began to Christianize. As the casting out of demons followed the gospel in Africa, the witch doctors began to lose their business to the "man of God."

## F. F. Bosworth

F. F. Bosworth was not known for exorcism, and there is little documentation on his involvement in deliverance that I have been able to find. However, his mention here is significant because he helped refine the Pentecostal theology, through an organized defense of the ministry of healing, in his book *Christ the Healer*, where Bosworth makes the case that healing is not only a charismatic miracle but also a part of the atonement. Therefore, anyone can receive healing by faith, like salvation.

Bosworth further served as a bridge between the Azusa generation and the revivalists of the 1950s, whom he influenced and at times mentored. If it was not for his writing, teaching, and men-

---

183 Allan Anderson, "Exorcism and the Conversion to African Pentecostalism," *Exchange* 35, no. 1 (January 2006): 116–33.

torship, the ministry and revelation regarding healing that started at Azusa may not have passed effectually to the next generation.

## Smith Wigglesworth

As supernatural ministry declined among Pentecostals, Smith Wigglesworth would arise and become one of the most famous and admired supernatural revivalists in early Pentecostalism. Unlike Bosworth and Lake, he was not influenced directly by Azusa Street but was introduced to healing at a revival service; it wasn't long before he began to lay hands on the sick and see healing as well.[184] His introduction to the Baptism of the Holy Spirit and tongues was slower but did come later at another Pentecostal meeting. His introduction to deliverance was much more personal.

Despite having already seen healing miracles in others, Wigglesworth fell ill and was unable to see recovery for himself. He recounts the following from *Ever Increasing Faith*:

> At one time I was so bound that no human power could help me. My wife was looking for me to pass away. There was no help. At that time I had just had a faint glimpse of Jesus as the Healer. For six months I had been suffering from appendicitis, occasionally getting temporary relief. I went to the mission of which I was pastor, but I was brought to the floor in awful agony, and they brought me home to my bed. All night I was praying, pleading for my deliverance, but none came. My wife was sure it was my home call and sent for a physician.

---

184 Liardon, *God's Generals: Why They Succeeded and Why Some Fail*, 206.

He said that there was no possible chance for me—my body was too weak. Having had the appendicitis for six months, my whole system was drained, and, because of that, he thought that it was too late for an operation. He left my wife in a state of brokenheartedness.

After he left, there came to our door a young man and an old lady. I knew she was a woman of real prayer. They come upstairs to my room. This young man jumped on the bed and commanded the evil spirit to come out of me. He shouted, "Come out you devil; I command you to come out in the name of Jesus!" There was no chance for an argument, or for me to tell him that I would never believe that there was a devil inside me. The thing had to go in the name of Jesus, and it went, and I was instantly healed.[185]

From that point forward, Wigglesworth began an aggressive campaign against the Devil. He taught that all sickness was satanic, and that some sicknesses could never be cured without exorcising spirits. Thus, when Wigglesworth would pray for the sick, he would adjure the Devil or an indwelling spirit to come out. He recounts in the same chapter several instances of praying for others with appendicitis, and "command[ing] the evil spirit to depart in the name of Jesus." Rebuking the Devil became his go-to formula for healing the sick.[186]

Exorcism was not second fiddle to healing in the ministry of Smith Wigglesworth; the two went nearly hand in hand. In addition

185 Smith Wigglesworth, *Ever Increasing Faith*, rev ed. (Springfield, MI: Gospel Publishing House, 1971), 19–20.
186 Wigglesworth, 18.

to always treating healing with exorcism, he understood demons to be responsible for false doctrine in the Church. In another example of exorcism in his book, Wigglesworth describes a *Christian* who was driven to insanity, repeating that he had committed the unpardonable sin. Wigglesworth recounts: "The Spirit of The Lord moved me to cry out, 'Come out, thou lying spirit.' In a moment, the evil spirit went and the man was free... The Lord said to me, 'This is what I baptized you for.'"[187]

Wigglesworth's form of exorcism was primarily charismatic, focusing on the elements of faith and power in the person driving out the demons. The exorcist could, at the same time, be the victim of demonization, and any Christian could liberate himself if he exercised faith; though the focus on the faith of the exorcist makes this still charismatic exorcism. From his writings, it seems that his exorcisms were generally very quick.

However, Wigglesworth had stronger forensic elements in his exorcism than his Pentecostal predecessors. He taught that sin was the root cause of bondage, thus repentance was a prerequisite to healing and deliverance. When Christians confess and repent, then faith "neither your sickness nor your sin will remain."[188] He further explained, "The Holy Ghost and the Word of God will bring to light every hidden, unclean thing that must be revealed. There is always a place of deliverance when you let God search out that which is spoiling and marring your life."[189] Persons afflicted by demons needed to get down to brass tacks about what caused their bondage in the first place, and deal with that in order to see free-

---

187  Wigglesworth, 13.
188  Wigglesworth, 37.
189  Wigglesworth, 19.

dom. In other places, we see Wigglesworth using a mild form of combative dialogue, asking a demonic power if it recognizes Christ came in the flesh, according to 1 John.[190]

## Conclusions

For early Pentecostals, the context of exorcism was secondary to healing and other supernatural manifestations. Exorcism stories are significantly less frequent than accounts of other miracles, especially healing. When exorcism did occur, it was most often connected with healing. For many of these early Pentecostals, laying hands on the sick and commanding healing was a form of exorcism, though it may not fit our typical model. Examples abound of a minister "exorcising" or "rebuking" sickness as one would a demon. Oral Roberts recounts that the obscure revivalist who prayed for him in the 1930s commanded tuberculous to "come out" as if it were a demon.[191]

Even at times when divine healing was practiced without typical exorcistic elements such as rebuking or exorcising, it was still seen as an exorcism in the sense that sickness was either the result of Satan's influence indirectly, or as a literal indwelling spirit. Healing was the most tangible way that early Pentecostals felt they could push back against Satan. Deafness and muteness were two infirmities that were more often than not thought to be the direct result of demons. We see this in the ministries of Azusa Street, Etter, and many others. The theological connection between sickness being Satan was what caused this fuzziness and overlap between healing and exorcism. Whenever Pentecostals wrote of a "healing," they could have been describing

---

190  Wigglesworth, 85.
191  Roberts Liardon, *God's Generals: The Healing Evangelists* (New Kensington, PA: Whitaker House, 2011), 165.

the healing of a demoniac. The term "deliverance" was also used very loosely, describing an act of God that liberated a person from something, whether that be demons, sickness, a mindset, an addiction, etc. It did not necessarily denote exorcism as it does today.[192]

Exorcism also sought to correct mental illness and religious error. Many of the accounts refer to people being exorcised who were in insane asylums or who displayed other mentally aberrant behavior, apparently corrected after being exorcised. Wigglesworth's account of the man who was persuaded he had committed the unpardonable sin is an excellent example of what this type of exorcism sought to resolve. Demons manifested themselves in false religious convictions that resulted in hopelessness and insane behavior.

The frequency and importance of exorcism proper can be seen as more *reactive* than *proactive*. Pentecostals did not often seek to exorcise anyone unless they showed signs of demonization. Besides the above situations, in crusades and revival meetings, exorcisms were normally in response to what Liardon refers to as a "growler," or someone displaying a demonic manifestation in the middle of the service. Early revivalists reacted to sickness, heresy, mental illness, and "growlers" manifesting in their meetings. And strangely enough, a lot of what we would consider demonic manifestation was attributed to the Holy Spirit moving in a person, rather than a demon.[193]

---

192 The blurring of terms was explained to me in an interview with Roberts Liardon.
193 Even today, in Pentecostal and charismatic meetings, there is debate over what sort of manifestations are demonic and which are divine. I was present in a meeting where a man began to make animalistic gestures and sexual moans. He was undisturbed for about ten minutes, as the manifestations intensified, and he ended up nearly on the ground grunting and growling. The leaders of this Church were unsure whether it was a demonic manifestation until his moans and screams made it impossible to ignore. He was than dragged in a back room, rebuked, and thrown out of the building. This sort of confusion about what constitutes a

## Ministry Deregulated

Classical Pentecostalism brought a significant deregulation to ministry in general, including exorcism. There was no designation on who could and who couldn't cast out demons. There was a vague sense in which those with charismatic power were typically the experts on the matter, but that power was displayed by experience, not designation. Despite this general sense, it seems to have been still fairly uncommon for lay Pentecostals to cast out demons. Lester Sumrall, who was converted in the Pentecostal Church in the 1930s, was surprised when he saw demonic manifestations overseas, and not in America.[194]

As early Pentecostalism lacked any systematic theology or teaching, it is difficult to answer where the general teaching was concerning the demonization of Christians. At Azusa Street, Christians were certainly exorcised; however, whether those exorcised were *baptized in the Holy Spirit* is a little more difficult to access. For Parham, conversion and the Baptism were no sure immunities against demonization, as those whom he exorcised after Azusa Street were all tongue-speaking Christians; For post-Azusa Pentecost, exorcism continued, but the focus of deliverance shifted more toward the Baptism of the Holy Spirit.

Pentecostals did exorcise many who were unbelievers as well. Most of the missionary exorcism that took place in Africa and Asia is assumed to be on unbelievers, though it wasn't always the case overseas either. Either way, the general conclusion was that Pen-

---

demonic manifestation seems to have been present in early Pentecostalism and continues today in their spiritual offspring.

194 Roberts Liardon, *God's Generals: The Healing Evangelists* (New Kensington, PA: Whitaker House, 2011), 116–117.

tecostals didn't spend any time delineating between believers and unbelievers when it came to casting out demons. When there was a delineation, it was with those who were baptized in the Holy Spirit.

## Style of Exorcism

Early Pentecostal exorcism emphasized brevity and simplicity: no questions, no ceremony, no scriptural recitation, or other elements of faith—spirits were expelled by command only. The process was often an oscillation between speaking in an "authoritative tongue" and commanding the spirits to leave in Jesus's name until the spirit was successfully expelled.[195] These classical Pentecostal exorcists used very few forensic elements either and measured deliverance by the cessation of demonic manifestation, or healing of a sickness, rather than the careful observation of forensic styles.

The clearest factor visible throughout early Pentecostal exorcism was *brevity*. Most descriptions of casting out demons give no other explanation than that an individual gave a command and the demons left. Sometimes there is some vagueness as to how much more took place than that, while other times, the accounts are clear about it being a "one and done" deal. Most often exorcisms were recorded as a command followed by quick deliverance. Sometimes more details were given. Laying on of hands was also sometimes employed, though distance was not considered an obstacle either. Some limited use of combative dialogue was used, but it was mostly limited to demanding the demon's name, and even this was not common.

---

195  This typical method was described by Dr. Liardon in an interview with the author and matches the general description of exorcism in primary documents of classical Pentecostalism.

## Factors of Change: Exorcism as Second Fiddle

In the revival of the supernaturalism of the early Pentecostal revivals, exorcism took second fiddle to healing and other charismatic experiences. Healing miracles were attention-grabbing and medically definable, contrasted with exorcism, which still probably had an air of mysticism in an age still deeply influenced by the Enlightenment.

Further, Exorcism was more controversial than healing. A healing miracle was very difficult to deny or be medically verified. Exorcism, on the other hand, is much more subjective. Demonic manifestations, loud rebukes, and authoritative tongues were all on the far end of the charismatic spectrum and did little to help alleviate the negative stigma around early Pentecostals, so it's easy to understand why exorcism did not take center stage.

## Pentecostal Power without Deliverance

The schism between Seymour and Parham probably represents one of the most unfortunate things to befall deliverance ministry. The schism represents not only a split in Pentecostalism but also a serious divergence in understanding of spiritual warfare. Seymour's school of thought was very tolerant of supernatural manifestations, generally assuming they were divine; this further led to exorcism being a primarily reactive charismatic miracle that was used to heal the insane or certain demonic illnesses. This school of thought would be the parent of Pentecostal and later charismatic understandings of exorcism throughout the next century. It was a secondary miracle that was primarily useful in asylums or missions. The Baptism of the Holy Spirit, and any manifestations that accompanied it, were of primary focus.

Parham's school of thought, which shared some similarities to *War on the Saints*, was more skeptical of supernatural manifestations, seeing the Baptism of the Holy Spirit in a stricter sense: an empowering experience evidenced by tongues. The demonic was seen as less overt in severe mental or physical illnesses, and more cunning, hiding in pride, religious error, and counterfeit supernatural experiences. With this, Parham's approach was more proactive, seeking to purify revival from demonic infiltration through exorcism, sound teaching, and protective measures. Unlike with Seymour, Parham's school of thought did not create a direct continuity with any movement or group in the Church. Despite little direction connection, the apparent heir to this approach would be the delivery ministries of the 1960s and '70s.

It is my opinion that the approach adopted by Seymour, which evolved into the general feeling of Pentecostal denominations, was the incorrect approach, that is reminiscent of previous redactions of deliverance from various revivals since the Reformation. The approach of highlighting supernaturalism without exorcism is dangerous, in that it does little to delineate itself from folk magic or paganism. Though there is much legitimate supernaturalism in the Pentecostal Churches, removing exorcism, or relegating it to a secondary, reactive ministry at best, opens the door to infiltration through counterfeit.

Further, by a judgment of results, this approach was not beneficial. As was the case in the previous chapters, exorcism was a source of major controversy, and once redacted, problems arose, and revivals began to collapse or lose continuity. Though correlation does not necessarily mean causation, I do not find it a coincidence that it was shortly after the expulsion of Parham that problems arose and Azusa collapsed, followed by the slow spiritual decline of Pentecostalism, and their eventual formation of denominations. Seymour had hoped to preserve the miracles at Azusa Street with an atmosphere of spiritual freedom, and instead, his successors lost much of their miraculous experience and fervor after deliverance was demoted.

In two generations, the spiritual offspring of Azusa would become some of the most avid opponents of the revival of deliverance ministry in the second half of the century, and still today, most Pentecostal denominations largely reject contemporary deliverance ministry for one reason or another. In the previous chapter, we saw the potential for Infant America to have experienced a revival of charismatic expression, and the great tragedy was that it was rejected. I believe that Azusa's rejection of the Parham approach to deliverance was as big of a blunder, delaying the general revival of deliverance for another hundred or more years.

# CHAPTER 9

# THE RESTORATION OF HEALING AND DELIVERANCE: THE OLD GUARD
## AD 1950-2000

By the 1950s, Pentecostals had organized into denominations and lost much of their revivalism. Further, Western Pentecostalism was avidly opposed to the demonization of Christians. The emphasis on the indwelling of the Holy Spirit merged with the Reformed doctrine common among protestants on the subject and solidified into the understanding that Christians could not have demons. By extension, exorcism was rarely the solution to demons, and either conversion, the Baptism of the Holy Spirit, or spiritual disciplines began the treatments.

The ministry of healing, while it remained theologically mainstream among Pentecostals, was still largely opposed by mainstream protestants. For the Pentecostal denominations, divine healing became more a matter of theology and saw less and less practical application.

The hostile environment toward healing and deliverance would set the stage for two renewal movements. The first movement was the Voice of Healing revivals of the 1950s and '60s, which would slowly and painfully bring healing to a greater degree of acceptance. The second movement would be a renewal of deliverance in the 1970s and '80s, which was by and large rejected by the Pentecostals and charismatics. Both movements represent a divergence in understanding of spiritual warfare that persists to this day.

Though the Voice of Healing was primarily focused on physical miracles, it did include a minor revival in exorcism as well, and that will primarily be the focus of our examination.

## The Voice of Healing Revival

In 1950, William Branham, who was already gaining traction as a healing evangelist, held a large crusade where he met F. F. Bosworth, who would join his ministry, connecting the new generation of revivalists to the generation of Azusa Street. It was around this time that Branham's ministry began to publish *The Voice of Healing* magazine to publicize and capture his revival events and healing miracles.[196]

Branham and his team, through their publication, would bring awareness to the reality of divine healing throughout the Church in the West. The renewal movement took divine healing from the back rooms of Pentecostal churches and into the limelight. Tent revivalism and charismatic preachers were the backbone of the revival; speakers would move around the country, set up shop, and display the power of God.

---

196 Liardon, *God's Generals: Why They Succeeded and Why Some Failed*, 329.

Like their predecessors, healing was the major emphasis of the revival. Stories and videos of tumors being slapped off the neck, cancers healed, legs lengthened, and incurable diseases being healed all circled like wildfire, giving tremendous excitement and energy to the movement. Thousands of people packed into tents with eager expectation, creating a powerful climate that revivalists could yield to make emotionally powerful altar calls and appeals toward repentance.

Exorcism was greatly eclipsed by the prominence of healing miracles, but it did take place, and the healing revivals played an important role in shaping how Pentecostals understand deliverance ministry today. William Branham, for example, was actually known for exorcism. Liardon describes him as identifying sin, sickness, and demons through divine revelation, and then dealing with them accordingly. Branham understood mental illness, doubt, lust, and emotional outbursts as the work of demons. Further, Branham's only conditions for healing or deliverance were a firm belief in God, and that he was a legitimate prophet.[197]

Roberts, Coe, and Allen, along with others, were less likely to use revelation to expel demons, over mere power encounters. Liardon described that at some tent revivals, severely demonized people would be tied to the tent poles until the preacher would lay hands on them for deliverance.[198] By and large, deliverance was primarily for the mentally ill, and some other extreme situations, and like the previous generation, healing took the role of prominence.

---

197 Liardon, 333.
198 Interview.

## The Collapse of the Voice of Healing Revival

Despite the tremendous power and spiritual energy created by the Voice of Healing, many of its leaders had major weaknesses, which resulted in the revival's collapse. The first issue was a lack of accountability. Each revivalist was a strongman over their own camp, with no peers to question or provide real feedback. Though they all had teams, these teams were more often yes-men than providers of serious accountability. At times when these revivalists were confronted with error, the confrontations were often ignored. Further, the lack of emphasis on scriptural literacy and strong theology created an open door to error.

By the late '50s, the revival began a terminal decline, with the collapse of various ministries. The first serious blow came with the death of Jack Coe in 1956 whose death was probably due to a combination of exhaustion, poor diet, and finally, polio.[199] By that time, Branham was already having major issues. With the loss of his manager, Gordon Lindsey, Branham succumbed to the influences of his cult personality, eventually claiming to be the great end times Elijah, a prophet of the dispensation. He then began to divine heretical new doctrines in order to reanimate his ministry and draw new attention.

By the '60s, with many of the original healing revivalists defunct, Oral Roberts and A. A. Allen became the frontliners. Branham responded with competitiveness, further declining his ministry into a cultish sect, denying the Trinity and eternal hell, and claiming that all women were the seed of Satan.[200] In 1965, he died in a car crash.

---

199 Liardon, *God's Generals: Why They Succeeded and Why Some Failed*, 374.
200 Liardon, 339.

## The Tragedy of A. A. Allen

Oral Roberts and A. A. Allen continued to carry the tent revival legacy into the 1960s. Throughout the decade, as revivalism cooled, Roberts moved from tent evangelism to televangelism and later, the building of a university. Roberts teaching and legacy, along with a number of others, would serve as the beginning of the Word of Faith movement, which in some ways was the successor to the Voice of Healing.

A. A. Allen, on the other hand, stayed in tent revivalism, and he slowly ventured further into exorcism than most of his peers had. As his ministry continued, deliverance rose to equal status of healing, and perhaps at times, even taking center stage. Allen went beyond the charismatic format of commanding demons out with some short, simple commands, and actually began to use some crude forms of interrogation.[201] Allen went so far as to publish pictures drawn by demoniacs and a tape recording of an interrogation of a demon.[202]

Allen's tactics and involvement in deliverance gained major opposition, ranging from the Ku Klux Klan to the Assemblies of God. Despite his incredible success in outliving the Voice of Healing, Allen's ministry began to decline as well, including lawsuits, family trouble, and declining health.

Allen was converted out of severe alcoholism, and as his health declined in his last years, at some point he relapsed. In 1970, he died of acute alcoholism. To summarize, the death was not a chronic, long-term drinking problem, but something more akin to a rapid overdose. It is the opinion of Dr. Liardon, to which I

---

201 This was probably more for showmanship than a forensic approach to exorcism.
202 Liardon, 402.

subscribe, that Allen was not a secret alcoholic throughout his ministry, but that he had a quick, though massive, relapse that killed him.[203]

## The Legacy of the Voice of Healing

One of the first things many people notice about the Voice of Healing is an incredible paradox in how some men could be used so greatly of God and have such terrible ends. Despite the major character flaws and failures, the Voice of Healing did basically make divine healing mainstream among continuationists. Now today, prayer for the sick and God's ability to heal are widely accepted, even if an understanding of faith for healing is not, and we have this revival in part to thank for that.

Despite this restoration, the Voice of Healing did not grow into an awakening that brought about a societal move toward God, as did the Great Awakenings of the previous centuries. The United States and the West continued in moral decline. Further, despite some involvement in exorcism, this revival did not bring deliverance to any degree of acceptance or understanding in the Church, beyond some mild acceptance in the Word of Faith.

Finally, how is it that men of God could have such tragic endings to ministry? Though it's certainly not the final say, my assessment is that these revivalists represented a threat to Satan's kingdom and were not adequately protected, due to theological issues, character flaws, a lack of accountability, and a lack of personal deliverance themselves.

---

203 Liardon, 405–409.

## The Deliverance Renewal

Between the Reformation and the 1960s, no continuity of deliverance tradition had been successfully established between two or more generations. Evangelism has had an unbroken continuity between the Monrovians and the current generation; the Baptism of the Holy Spirit has had a continuity since Azusa, and healing at least since the 1950s, if not sooner. However, in every revival or movement in which exorcism played some role, it was somehow or another aborted before reaching the next generation.

The first generation of "deliverance ministers" all describe how they struggled to find literature and teaching on how to cast out demons. Though there were some examples, as we have examined in previous chapters, much of this was obscure, difficult to find, and did not provide much light on how to actually deal with demons. This generation would be the first to write their experiences and methodologies (that wouldn't be redacted), thus establishing a continuity between themselves and the current generation.

All of the schools of thought about deliverance ministry among evangelicalism today can be traced back to five persons, which I call the "Old Guard"—namely, Lester Sumrall, Derek Prince, Frank Hammond, Bob Larson, and Win Worley. Though there were other prominent deliverance ministers in this generation, these five were the most influential in establishing schools of thought, and others, even if they were more well known, would typically fall into one of these categories.

### Lester Sumrall

Lester Sumrall first encountered demons in 1936 while on an overseas mission. During a crusade, a young girl started writhing on the floor, and after being rebuked, sat still with a deathly stare. While Sumrall preached, he prayed and contemplated what to do about the situation. After his sermon, he rebuked the demon and the girl was instantly released from her trance, with no diagnostic dialogue or laying on of hands.[204]

Sumrall would later encounter more demons and exorcism throughout his ministry, both overseas and in the West. The most famous of these situations came in the early '50s when a girl in the Philippines was being bitten by demons. Police, doctors, and guards all saw the bites but were unable to do anything about it. Recordings of the girl's screams and descriptions of the bites were broadcast over the radio, as the government requested help dealing with the situation. The only Christian to answer the call, promising deliverance, was Sumrall. For three days, he battled the demons through rebuke, prayer, and fasting until she was finally delivered from the agony. The sensational account opened the door for some of the first protestant crusades in the country.[205]

Sumrall did not represent an innovation of deliverance thought, but rather a revival of the strangulated Pentecostal tradition of exorcism, receiving influences primarily from Wigglesworth. His approach was very basic, similar to Voice of Healing and early Pentecostal revivalists: quick, commands, normally only vocal. The Sumrall school of thought was that demons needed to respond immediately, and leave with a command, if the man of God was truly anointed and had enough faith. In very severe circumstances, such as the girl bitten by demons, prolonged fasting may be required to dislodge demons. Sumrall's approach was a firmly

204 Liardon, *God's Generals: The Healing Evangelists*, 116–117.
205 Liardon, 130–135.

charismatic approach to exorcism; the elements of importance lay primarily in the minister, that being faith and anointing.

Sumrall did, however, bring spiritual warfare further than the Voice of Healing revivalists. Demons caused more than severe mental issues and issues of gross sin. Demons could cause simple emotional episodes in otherwise pious Christians and other more subtle issues glossed over by previous Pentecostals. Sumrall taught that demonization was widespread in the Church, and that the lack of availability of deliverance was a major problem.[206]

Sumrall's school of thought was most purely continued by Norvel Hayes and a handful of others who maintained the necessity of deliverance as a frontline ministry. When contemporary Pentecostal groups accept deliverance, it is typically a continuation of the Sumrall understanding, and it also finds some continuation in the Word of Faith. These various groups at times had their own version of his teaching, but they basically share the core school of thought. Despite some influence of deliverance in these groups, they still largely defaulted back to the traditional Pentecostal rejection of deliverance, as something that took place rarely, quickly, and hopefully overseas.

## Derek Prince

In 1953, Derek Prince was suffering from chronic depression. It was a depression he was familiar with since most of the men in his family had a similar condition. However, after he was born again, he sought to be free. He fasted, he prayed, he read the scripture, which brought only temporary relief before the cloud would return with a vengeance.

---

206 For a complete understanding of Sumrall's Deliverance Theory, see: Lester Sumrall, "Demons and Deliverance" (YouTube, 1982).

Finally, while reading the scripture one day, Prince saw the term "spirit of heaviness" in Isaiah 61:3. It occurred to him that the depression was not at all a part of his personality that needed to be "reckoned dead" (Rom. 6:11), but rather an alien spirit that had taken up residence in his personality. Upon this realization, Prince called on God for deliverance, and describes a pressure being released from his chest and a dramatic change in his mental health following.[207]

Prince withheld this experience for ten years, due to embarrassment and the popular doctrine that taught against the demonization of Christians. That changed in 1963 when Prince was approached by a charismatic Baptist pastor. The pastor enlisted Prince's help in dealing with a demonized woman from his congregation. Prince explains that the woman passed every litmus test for the legitimacy of her salvation and was baptized in the Holy Spirit. Despite this, she manifested demons that verbally confronted Prince and were eventually expelled.[208] Shortly after this, while Prince was preaching at his church, his worship leader had a violent demonic manifestation. Ironically, his Pentecostal members were all in a state of shock, and charismatic Presbyterians were the ones who came to his aid and expelled the spirits.[209] After this, streams of people began to come to Prince looking for deliverance from demons, and the father of modern deliverance was born.

In contrast to Sumrall, Prince represented a divergence in deliverance theory from the classical Pentecostal understanding and approach. In some sense, the other schools of thought can

---

207 Derek Prince, *They Shall Expel Demons* (Grand Rapids, MI: Chosen Books, 1998), 30–33.
208 Prince, 43–45.
209 Prince, 52.

be broadly categorized with Prince under the term "forensic" as opposed to the charismatic approach of Sumrall and other Pentecostals. Outside of the realm of exorcism, Prince would rise to become a very influential theologian through radio, itinerate preaching, and a prolific bibliography. The sermons and literature Prince produced ensured a deliverance continuity after his death.

Derek Prince was above all things a teacher. The word that was translated teacher in Ephesians 4:11 is the Greek word for which we get the words "doctor" and "doctrine."[210] In other words, it means a doctor of theology. As Augustine, among others, was considered a Doctor of early Christian theology, so Prince would prove to be the doctor of deliverance theology. He was the first, as far as my research has uncovered, to give a detailed theological framework to spiritual warfare. The rest of the deliverance renewal would operate, more or less, out of this theological framework that Prince developed.

That theological framework explained the demonization of Christians, how demons gain entry into the personality, the problems they cause, and how they can be expelled. The points of entry and symptoms of demonization were much more extensive than the understanding of the Pentecostal tradition. Rather than the mentally ill and grossly iniquitous, demonization as seen by Prince included most Christians, to some degree or another.[211]

Though some previous exorcists throughout Church history had what I call a "forensic" approach to exorcism, Prince was the first who had a recorded, systematic approach to casting out demons. What primarily differentiated it from charismatic exorcism was that the primary issue was not the faith or gift of the exor-

210  Strong's G1320: *didáskalos*.
211  Prince, *They Shall Expel Demons*, 165–192.

cist; rather, the person being delivered must meet certain conditions to receive deliverance from God. For Prince, these conditions were (1) the New Birth, (2) humility, (3) confession and repentance of sin, (4) forgiveness of any offense, (5) a total renunciation and break with the occult, (6) breaking of curses (which could include negative words spoken over a person, or generational curses started from occultism), (7) a firm stance of faith, and (8) demons must be forcefully commanded to leave—expelled.[212]

The legacy of Prince would be that framework in which the others would build and expand their schools of thought in various ways. There are some that will generally accept Prince's school of thought only, and this includes some charismatics and deliverance ministries today.

## Frank Hammond

Frank Hammond was a Baptist pastor who was introduced to the supernatural at a Kathryn Kuhlman meeting. After witnessing hundreds of people healed from various infirmities, his heart yearned to see one of his colleagues in ministry healed from chronic migraines. Taking the matter to prayer, Hammond felt the Lord revealed to him that the problem was demonic. After overcoming his consternation, he told his friend what he'd heard. The colleague insisted that Hammond expel the spirit from him. Finally, Hammond and he prayed together, and after several rebukes, the man went into a coughing fit and was cured. As of the writing of *Pigs in the Parlor*, the man hadn't had any migraines.[213]

---

212 Prince, 216.
213 Frank Hammond and Ida Mae Hammond, *Pigs in the Parlor: A Practical Guide to Deliverance* (Kirkwood, MO: Impact Books, 1973), 105–109.

After this, like Prince, Hammond was flooded with people looking for deliverance from demons and would become fairly well known for this ministry. At some point, Derek Prince contacted him and recommended that he write a book on deliverance ministry, which led to the publication of *Pigs in the Parlor*. When it was first published at the prime of the charismatic renewal, it spread like wildfire, being one of the most widely circulated books on deliverance and reaching most of the charismatic world. The effect would be a general awareness that "casting out demons" was something that happened at certain times in charismatic meetings. Despite its wide circulation, Hammond's defense of the demonization of Christians, and his estimation that every Christian needs some degree of deliverance,[214] these concepts would be either ignored or opposed by most in the charismatic Churches.

Hammond was not a scholar like Prince, but a small-town pastor. Despite his authorship and itinerate ministry, the pastoral perspective always colored his approach to deliverance. He basically operated in the same theological framework as Prince and appeared to defer to him as his senior.[215] His deliverance methodology did expand, and his school of thought would become something independent of the framework of Prince.

After the publication of *Pigs in the Parlor*, Hammond was not at first involved in any itinerate deliverance ministry. He was contacted by Win Worley, who wrote another deliverance book, *Battling the Hosts of Hell*, shortly after Hammond published his book.

---

214 Hammond and Hammond, 22.
215 Hammond and Hammond, 170–171. Hammond appears to defer to Don Basham and Derek Prince as his seniors in deliverance, at least at the writing of *Pigs in the Parlor*.

Worley invited him to be involved in his growing itinerate platform, and they began to travel and minister together for a period of time in the 1970s. As they each got busier, this relationship faded, and both went in their own directions, devolving different approaches to deliverance ministry.[216]

The most well-known and significant advancement from Hammond was the "Schizophrenia revelation," which would have some influence on most contemporary deliverance ministries. The revelation taught that possessing demons worked in tandem with one another to create a certain mental or emotional condition in the person they tormented. These little companies of spirits had an organizational structure, plan, and ways to avoid or recover from attempted exorcism. If Hammond's theory was correct, the simple methods of Sumrall and Prince may not always be effective.

Hammond further devolved a "revelatory-forensic" approach to exorcism that relied heavily on revelatory gifts in the deliverance ministry to supernaturally discern these demonic structures and so dispossess them. Beyond revelating specific spirits and their rights to invade, the method of expulsion was also very simple, basic commands, speaking in tongues, etc. Hammond was avidly opposed to allowing demons to speak at all, whether in combative dialogue or any other form, believing this to be mediumistic.[217] He further expanded upon the understanding of deliverance as a process of breakthrough and a part of the Christian's sanctification, rather than a single charismatic experience. In addition to

---

216 According to an interview with Michael Thierer, the pastor of Hegewisch Baptist Church (May 2023).
217 According to an interview with Bob Larson (June 2021) and remarks in several of Hammond's sermons.

this, Hammond developed more specialized teachings in many of his books, including deliverance ministry with children, and how to overcome specific character flaws such as a rejected mentality.

Hammond's approach is also typically embraced by charismatic groups that accept deliverance and finds its home in many "deliverance teams" in charismatic Churches in the West. These generally have a milder form of deliverance that is practiced in private, appointment-type sessions, rather than in public meetings, contrasted with the more public approach of the previous two schools of thought.

### Bob Larson

Bob Larson was first confronted with demonism while traveling in third world countries as a student in 1967. These bizarre and supernatural manifestations sparked his interest in the supernatural and caused him to question why it apparently didn't happen in the West. Shortly after this time, he began full-time ministry.[218] In 1971, at a Youth for Christ rally in St. Louis, Larson was approached by a teenager who claimed to have sex with the Devil. Larson and another minister prayed for the girl, and after a few failed attempts, provoked a manifestation. Larson began to interrogate the demon, asking for its name first, what other demons are present, how they entered, etc. After this, he led the girl through the sinner's prayer, forced the demon to self-imprecate, and expelled it.[219]

Bob Larson would quickly become a popular speaker in the 1970s through radio evangelism and prolific writing. His primary

---

218  Bob Larson, *Larson's Book of Spiritual Warfare* (Nashville, TN: Thomas Nelson, 1999), 12.
219  Larson, 17–25.

focus during this time was more exposure of the occult and Satanism. At first, he maintained the popular theological position that Christians could not be demonized. Larson explains that this position was devoid of scriptural backing and was based on the echo chamber of evangelical Christian leaders. It took some overwhelming circumstances to finally change his mind:

> I overcame this theological prejudice when I agreed to pray with a woman named Audrey. She claimed to be a Christian, but said she had demons. I thought perhaps Audrey wasn't sure what it meant to be a Christian. During our discussion several demons manifested. One was a spirit of death. It overtook her, and she looked as though she were comatose. She was lying rigidly on the floor with her hands stiff against her sides . . . . Her pulse slowed until she only wheezed small spurts of breath. I believed that she was going to die if we didn't intervene . . . . I was puzzled. How could a Christian have a demon and be pushed to the point of death? . . . I interrogated the demon. "What part of her do you possess?"
>
> "I don't have her spirit, that belongs to God. But I do have her body. I entered into her before she became a Christian, when she was involved in the occult."[220]

After this experience, Larson describes seeking the scripture and finding little real evidence against the demonization of Christians in the New Testament.[221] Larson would go on to become well

---

220 Larson, 326.
221 Larson, 327.

known for the countercult movement and exorcism through his radio ministry, and throughout the '90s, he shifted his focus primarily to exorcism. Up until today, Larson has continued in full-time deliverance ministry, and he represents the last living member of the five we examine in this chapter.

Larson's school of thought would develop into a hyper-forensic approach, which looked to discover the source of demonization and their legal rights in as much detail as possible. According to Larson's methodology, most demonization begins not with personal sin, but generational curses, that were often started a long time ago by serious witchcraft, murder, or other heinous sin. These curses then carry their load of demons with them, generation to generation, until someone is properly delivered. Breaking these generational curses is essential to the Larson school of thought, and any deliverance that doesn't surgically discover and break these curses is sloppy, and perhaps useless. In order to break these curses, the minister must obtain as much detail as possible about its origin: the side of the family, how long ago it started, and what event initiated the curse.[222]

Larson's total approach to deliverance emphasized the need to gather as much information as possible, beginning with a detailed interview of the ministry recipient in order to gain an understanding of the infrastructure of the demonization. Once a vague sketch is produced, the exorcist is to provoke a demonic manifestation and bring the spirits through a thorough interrogation in order to fill in any missing pieces. Once all the information has been acquired, the recipient is led through repentance and curse breaking. Then, the

---

222 Bob Larson, *Curse Breaking* (Shippensburg, PA: Destiny Image, 2013).

exorcist will force the demon to verbally pronounce its defeat and expulsion. Larson's school of thought represents the most methodical and systematic approach to exorcism and deliverance, of the five.

In contrast to Hammond's reliance on revelatory gifts, Larson's school of thought sees words of knowledge and prophetic gifts to occasionally be helpful, but highly subjective and unreliable, and thus understands them to be supplementary.[223] Larson would also introduce tactics of spiritual pressure to force demons to comply with commands. It is unclear whether this concept was first developed by Worley or Larson, but both groups would use such tactics to torment demons, though in very different ways. If spirits did not respond to the commands of the minister, then pressures would be applied, such as scripture reading, prayer, and invocation of angelic assistance. In his post-radio deliverance ministry, Larson would eventually adopt the use of a cross, similar to practices of liturgical exorcism, the use of a Bible as a "sword" to strike demons, along with anointing oil.

Unlike his peers, Larson takes a deeper look at the relationship between mental illness and demonization. The traditional Pentecostal approach was that the two were synonymous to some degree. The deliverance renewal did not change that approach much, other than perhaps seeing mental illness as an especially complex web of demonic bondage. Larson, and later Dr. Ed Murphy, took the position that mental illness and demons were entirely different, though they sometimes overlapped. The Larson school of thought basically recognizes the validity of modern psychology, though understood it to be severely limited by itself.[224]

---

223  Bob Larson, *Dealing with Demons* (Shippensburg, PA: Destiny Image, 2016), 11–12.
224  Larson, 114.

The mental illness with which Larson is most concerned is dissociative identity disorder (DID), formerly known as multiple personality disorder (MPD). As Larson understands it, a person can have a fractured personality, in which several "alter" egos can be present. Demonization can occur in the "core" of a personality, or in one or more of these "alters," and demons present in alters need to be dealt with accordingly. Larson's approach to restoring these fractured alters is a type of healing that deals with the trauma that originated the fracture.[225]

Larson's methodology, and those who follow his school of thought today, represents a very refined and highly forensic approach to deliverance that emphasizes the importance of detail. Since his experience in exorcism now spans over fifty years, that has given plenty of time to develop, refine, and improve the investigatory and forensic style of exorcism.

Many contemporary leaders in deliverance attest a continuation of Larson's legacy, though in my observation, few of them use much of his methodology. However, Larson's school of thought is continued in the many deliverance ministries that are connected to him through his school and network, and there are some larger ministries that largely maintain his approach.

### Win Worley

"I stared into the eyes of the young man; and the demon glared back, blazing defiance and rage. His face had gone white and twisted so that it scarcely appeared

---

225 Larson's teaching on DID is interspersed in his writing. This information is taken from his instructional course, International School of Exorcism, Level 3, Course 3, 2014.

human. When we proceeded, insisting and praying in Jesus' name for the demon's defeat, he began to roar with unbelievable volume."[226]

In December of 1970, Baptist pastor Win Worley was baptized in fire, with a grueling six-hour exorcism, where he battled incredibly violent demons in a young man. The demons were vocal, violent, and defiant, steadfastly refusing to leave, until Worley finally broke down all their defenses though whatever he could find tormented the demons.[227]

The grueling, pitched battle between the servants of Christ and the Host of Hell would be the hallmark of Worley's approach to deliverance. After this initial exorcism, Worley would be confronted with a wave of demonized believers, inside and outside of his church. He kept a journal of these events that would be published as *Battling the Hosts of Hell* in 1976, giving Worley a much larger audience. Though he would not grow to the same degree of influence as the previous four ministers we have examined, he would contribute the most extensive demonology of the Old Guard.

Early in his ministry, Worley felt that the Lord revealed to him that deliverance was an "unfolding revelation" that would go beyond simply casting out demons and eventually culminate in a great revival. Over the course of his twenty-three-year deliverance ministry, his theory on spiritual warfare would go far beyond simple exorcism and encompass a large realm of spiritual warfare.

---

226 Win Worley, *Battling the Hosts of Hell* (Mesquite, TX: WRW Publications, 1976), 15.
227 Worley, 14–16.

Worley, his church, and his sphere of influence would operate like a laboratory. A hypothesis would be proposed either from something found in scripture or used in an exorcism; it would be peer-reviewed to see whether it had any scriptural allusion or reference and tested in ministry. If it passed these tests, the information would be published in the latest of Worley's books or booklets. Though the other members of the Old Guard all developed extensively throughout their ministries, especially the highly refined approach of Larson, Worley's school of thought was able to expand and encompass much more than his peers, due to this larger research system. A general progression of revelation can be followed throughout his years of ministry, and we will briefly sketch this progression.

*Tormenting, Interrogating, and Expelling Demons:* The foundation of Worley's methodology was the fierce, pitched battle. Like Prince, the Worley theory saw a sense of meeting God's conditions for deliverance, though simply meeting these conditions was not always enough. Demons must be forcibly evicted. The Worley School emphasized the necessity of demonic manifestations in deliverance. Interrogation was not only for information about legal rights and points of entry, but a psychological breakdown and a form of torture and humiliation, similar to what MacMullen called "manhandling of demons."[228] This interrogation could also procure information about Satan's plans for a region, ministry, or even the world. Throughout the ministry, this theory would develop an extensive number of tools to torment and pressure demons, including angelic invocation, imprecatory scriptures, agape love, songs about hell, humiliating threats and jokes, and more.

---

228 Ramsay MacMullen, *Christianizing the Roman Empire*, 27.

*Witchcraft Curses:* It was discovered, when after severely tormenting a spirit of lust, that certain demons could not leave because of a curse, either from witchcraft or negative words spoken over a person in ignorance. At times, curses needed to be discovered and broken.[229] This understanding of curses differed slightly from Larson's approach.

*Binding Demons:* Initially in deliverance, it was thought that once demons were manifesting, deliverance workers needed to fight until they were expelled. It was discovered that they could "bind" or subdue the demons temporarily and resume the deliverance later. This concept was expanded to include binding demons in persons through intercessory prayer.[230]

*Loosing Angelic Spirits:* Worley later expanded the principle of binding to include "loosing" or invoking angelic assistance in deliverance and intercessory prayer. An intercessor could "loose" specific spirits (a spirit of peace, a spirit of wisdom, etc.) to fulfill a specific need, or a deliverance worker could "loose" an angel to assist in a deliverance. This theory did not understand Christians as having authority over angels but invoking their activity through the Lord.[231]

*Intercessory Binding and Loosing:* Eventually, this concept was expanded to include binding and loosing with principalities and powers in the heavenlies. Worley began to encourage Christians to bind demonic powers in the heavens and loose God's angels to combat them. According to Worley, this was the most effectual and potent form of spiritual warfare.[232]

---

229 Win Worley, "Curse Breaking," 1978.
230 Win Worley, "How to Bind and Loose," 1983.
231 Win Worley, "Loosing the Spirits of God," 1980.
232 Win Worley, *Warfare Prayers* (Mesquite, TX: WRW Publications, 2013).

*Sins of the Fathers:* This was Worley's perspective on generational curses, and it developed differently from Larson's theory. Worley's theory taught that patterns of sinful behavior, and their accompanying demons, were passed on generationally. Once the pattern was identified and repented of, the curse was broken, and a person could gain a degree of freedom, though the demons would still need to be expelled. Contrast Larson's theory, which emphasized the importance of gaining exact details, which would need to come by interrogating a demon.[233]

*The Fragmented Soul:* Worley taught that the soul consisted of willpower, mental capacity, and emotional capacity. According to this theory, the forces of hell could fragment parts of the soul, and thus diminish the above capacities. This fragmentation could take place through trauma, witchcraft, substance abuse, soul ties, and certain kinds of demonically charged music. The solution involved "loosing" angels to recover the fragmented parts and restore them, while expelling any spirits occupying the fragmented part.[234]

*The Alcoholic Syndrome:* This syndrome refers to a pattern of emotional dysfunction that typically will manifest in substance abuse, though it can exist without it. It basically understands addiction as one facet of a network of emotional dysfunction and relational dysfunction, with a wide variety of spirits that need to be expelled in order to bring relief. The Worley school of thought understood that this syndrome could be passed on generationally without a person actually ever being addicted to drugs or alcohol.[235]

233 Win Worley, "Sins of the Fathers," 1982.
234 Win Worley, "The Fragmented Soul," 1982.
235 Win Worley, "The Alcoholic Syndrome," 1985.

Of further note, Worley also popularized a new model of exorcism. Rather than expelling demons out of individuals, he would lead an entire congregation or group through a series of standardized repentances and prayers, and then rebuke a laundry list of demons out of the entire group, often called a "mass deliverance."

## Deliverance Revivalists Compared and Contrasted

| Revivalist | Lester Sumrall | Derek Prince | Frank Hammond | Bob Larson | Win Worley |
|---|---|---|---|---|---|
| Theological Background | Classical Pentecostal; itinerate evangelist and missionary. | Pentecostal; itinerate teacher; scholarly background. | Charismatic Baptist; pastor and author. | Evangelical; itinerate evangelist, radio show host and author. | Southern Baptist; pastor. |
| Approach to Exorcism | Missional exorcism: highly charismatic approach based on faith/anointing of exorcist. Exorcisms are very brief and simple. | Moderately forensic: emphasizing God's conditions for receiving deliverance. | Revelatory-forensic: use of revelatory gifts to discover demons and their grounds, to dislodge them. | Highly forensic: based largely on meeting conditions of repentance with as much specificity as possible. | Charismatic-forensic: exorcism involves meeting conditions of repentance. Factors of spiritual strength of demons and exorcists. |

| Prolifer-ation of Demons | Many people, including Christians, need deliv-erance, but less in Chris-tianized nations. | Most Christians need some degree of deliv-erance. Unbeliev-ers not entitled to deliver-ance. | All Christians need some degree of deliv-erance. Unbeliev-ers not entitled to deliver-ance. | Most Christians need some degree of deliv-erance. Unbeliev-ers may at times receive deliver-ance. | All people need various degrees of deliv-erance. Unbeliev-ers not entitled to deliver-ance. |
|---|---|---|---|---|---|
| Legacy | John G. Lake min-istries, et al., Word of Faith under-standing of exor-cism. | Most deliverance ministers today attribute influence to Prince. | Char-ismatic ministries involved in deliver-ance often use this school of thought. | Larson has teams of ministers trained in this school of thought. Use of auto-im-precation. | Use of mass deliv-erance can be traced to Worley. Various Bapticostal Churches trace their deliverance legacy to Worley. |
| Impressum | *Demons: The Answer Book* *Courage to Conquer* *Et al.* | *They Shall Expel Demons* *Blessings and Curses* *Et al.* | *Pigs in the Parlor* *Obstacles to Deliver-ance* *Et al.* | *Larson's book of Spiritual Warfare* Interna-tional School of Exorcism | *Battling the Hosts of Hell,* & *Hosts of Hell* series |

## Needless Casualties?

Derek Prince and Win Worley both pioneered, in different ways, a belief that Christians can shape the course of history by engaging principalities and powers in the heavenlies.[236] Worley's primary tool for this was "binding and loosing," which we examined in the previous section, while Prince taught more on fasting and intercessory prayer, generally. This belief became popular, and perhaps even spread more than deliverance ministry proper during their time.

Later, John Paul Jackson would publish *Needless Casualties of War*, with the premise that attacking principalities and powers was useless and would only result in devastating counterattacks. His thesis was based on a vision he had, and a litany of horror stories of Christians who attempted to attack principalities, and then backslid or died. Jackson's view of the matter would become the overwhelming mainstream view for the last twenty years, even among advocates of deliverance ministry proper. It is my opinion that Jackson's premise is based on experience, rather than sound theology, and represents another abortion of proper spiritual warfare theology.

## The End of the Old Guard

The generation of deliverance revivalists from the '60s and '70s would eventually pass away, and despite their great effort and contribution, exorcism would not become widely accepted by the Church. Pentecostal and charismatic Christianity remained especially hostile toward them. Derek Prince and Don Basham were anathemized by several major Pentecostal denominations, including the Assemblies of God, which threatened to pull the papers of any pastor who accepted the demonization of Chris-

---

236 That is, high-ranking satanic forces that control nations and regions, rather than possess persons.

tians. Win Worley was resisted by his native Southern Baptist Convention. By and large, all of the deliverance revivalists were highly resisted by denominational Christianity, and their work would remain fringe.

Though they fought for it, the great deliverance revival would not come during their time. All of the members of this generation, with the exception of Larson, have passed away. Why did they not see a revival, like many of the other great moves that we have examined so far? In my estimation, there are three major reasons that prevented a general revival of deliverance.

The first is that these leaders lacked any connection to the literature, teachings, mistakes, and successes of a previous generation. Though exorcism was common during certain periods as we have seen, there was never an establishment of continuity through a body of literature and teaching. The initial years of this generation were spent "flying blind" and developing that very body of teaching.

The second issue is that, like evangelism, the Baptism of the Holy Spirit, and divine healing, deliverance ministry had major theological barriers to overcome. The difference is that these other renewals had several generations to overcome these barriers, and that deliverance is by far more resisted than any other ministry by the Kingdom of Darkness. We have now seen generation after generation of that determined and fierce resistance to a revival of deliverance. The fact is that a renewal of deliverance is just more resisted than a revival of any other kind.[237]

---

237 Dr. Liardon shared this opinion, that even as deliverance becomes more mainstream, it will remain as highly resisted as it has been, representing the most direct threat to the Kingdom of Darkness.

The third issue is that these leaders lacked unity. Other than some sporadic exceptions, they did not work together, and at times were not even on good terms with each other. Each leader and his school of thought was basically independent of the others. This lack of unity was a major weakness of this generation, and I believe it's the hurdle we must overcome in our day.

CHAPTER 10

# CONCLUSIONS:
## REVIVE OR REDACT?

I n the course of twenty centuries, we have demonstrated in this study a common theme of revival and redaction of the ministry of exorcism. Exorcism has its roots firmly in the ministry of Christ and the apostles, and it was understood by the writers of the New Testament to be a normal part of Church life. In Christ's day, his exorcisms led the Pharisees to the blasphemous claim that his ministry was powered by black magic. In the days of the apostles, they were resisted, at times, specifically because of exorcism (Acts 16:16–24). Despite this resistance, it was a major and enduring aspect of Christian ministry from the apostolic age, up through the early centuries of the Church.

In the first three centuries of the Church, exorcism remained a cardinal aspect of Christian ministry and a leading cause of the conversion of the Roman Empire. Without it, healing miracles and natural evangelism would likely have not yielded the same results. Even as other charismatic expressions declined in the late second century, exorcism continued. In the post-Nicene Church, it remained common enough for Augustine and Chrysostom to refer to it almost casually as a part of Church life.

As the Church declined into the Middle Ages, exorcism became ritualized, trivialized, and finally disappeared altogether. When it returned, it was in a perverted, magical form that did not resemble the deliverance ministry of the Gospels. Only the faint tradition of baptismal exorcism remained as a relic from the ministry of the early Church, and that, too, ritualized beyond comparison with the Gospels. In my opinion, the decline of legitimate exorcism, and the decline of availability of the scriptures, were two primary causes of the decline of the medieval Church into the gross darkness of corruption.

At the protestant Reformation, it appears the Spirit of God attempted to revive the *full* Gospel, including exorcism. However, Reformed Christians, in their misguided zeal, went too far, in reforming exorcism right out of the protestant Church, and in combating Catholic magic, excluded legitimate supernatural workings of God's Spirit. Exorcism, along with most charismatic expression, was struck out of the Reformation.

At every revival since then, deliverance made a comeback, and every time, it was redacted, covered up, resisted, and hidden. Fox and Wesley, now typically thought of as great men of God, were resisted with vitriol, in part because they cast out demons. When they died, their successors covered up the evidence, and hid the records, so no one could know the dark shame of deliverance. The Puritan Mather fasted, and prayed, and confronted darkness in a deliverance ministry, and yet, he was swallowed up in the witchcraft debacle, which led to his libel and slander, along with a complete eclipse of deliverance miracles.

Deliverance was rejected by the revival at Azusa Street, after the controversy with Parham; shortly after that rejection, the revival imploded, and Pentecostalism has generally been hostile toward deliverance ministry since then, with some noteworthy exceptions. Deliverance popped up briefly in the Voice of Healing and made a more determined effort to return to the Church in the charismatic renewal. Despite the most literature and teaching on it produced by a single generation, it was resisted and rejected by the majority of the Church, and we have seen no major, national revival since then.

Though this study is not exhaustive enough to draw firm conclusions, I would like to make some tentative observations on what could be covered:

1. A proactive deliverance ministry seems to be connected with the success of revivalism or decline of the Church. Generally, where there was some exorcism, there was successful evangelism and a guard against corruption of revival. Where this critical ministry was removed, often it seems that decline followed.

2. Regardless of our theological positions, exorcism has been a consistent attribute of Christian ministry of the Church. The period in which it was least common, the High Middle Ages, is also the period most of us would want to replicate the least. But for the greater part, it seems to have existed in some capacity throughout the history of the Church and represents an accepted part of the Great Tradition of Christianity.

a. Exorcism was also consistently *resisted* after the Reformation. Despite always returning, it was resisted and fought viciously, often due to the theological framework set up by Calvinism.

b. Before the Reformation, there was never a theological challenge to deliverance; however, there was a gradual decline away from forensic and charismatic exorcism and toward ritual exorcism, and later magic. That decline ran parallel to a general decline in the Church.

3. Deliverance always existed in both the Church and in mission. There are some who would argue that exorcism should only take place in the Church, or only in the highways and byways. Christ fought demons in the synagogue and in the tombs; for the most part, those who did cast out demons followed his example, and deliverance has always taken place in the Church, and in mission. There is, therefore, no *historical* basis for excluding deliverance to only the lost or only the Church.

4. The teaching that denies the possibility of Christians being demonized is a theological novelty, and rather unorthodox when compared with the general trend of the Christian Church. Before Calvin, this research could not find any theologian or writer who flatly taught that Christians could not have demons. Some writers suggested that there was deliverance at conversion, but this does not carry over. Any time where the subject was up for discussion in the first fifteen centuries, the jury was that Christians could have demons. After the Reformation, despite Calvin's influence, a great number of persons still taught that

Christians at times needed deliverance from demons, including Fox, Mather, Wesley, et al. Therefore, it is more a novelty to teach that Christians *cannot* be demonized. Those who uphold this doctrine have history against them. If they search the scripture for evidence of that position, they may see why so few of the great minds in the Church held that position.

5. Orthodox deliverance ministry was always *public*. The concept of private exorcism was developed with the office of exorcist and more firmly solidified by the Catholic Church, especially during the Enlightenment. This superstitious practice of hiding exorcism in back rooms and basements is the carryover of a Catholic understanding of exorcism.

6. The most successful form of exorcism is that which is *proactive*; that is, actively seeking to dispossess demons from people, both in the Church and in mission. *Reactive* exorcism, that is, reacting to a clearly demonic manifestation, is not as beneficial, but still better than a *reactive* approach. The kingdom of Satan appears to work in subtlety and hiddenness. If the Church waits only for him to expose himself, we give him a great advantage.

7. Exorcism, when at its most healthy, was practiced by a large number of lay Christians to some degree. At times when it was confined to clergy, exorcists, or specially called persons, it was much less effective in its impact.

Today, the Church in the West is confronting more demonism and darkness than perhaps at any other point. From a historical perspective, deliverance ministry is a primary weapon to be used to fight against such demonism, and yet, we in the Western Church have consistently handicapped ourselves and robbed ourselves of one of the most effective tools in combating paganism and demonism. If we expect to see any sort of revival on a national scale, I believe it must be preceded by a general acceptance and practice of deliverance in the Church.

As to the demonization of Christians, it is beyond the scope of this work to argue that point theologically, and that has been done elsewhere effectively. But from a historical and logical perspective, it is detrimental. If Christians can in fact be demonized, those who teach to the contrary do the Devil's work in helping him hide himself while he destroys lives, drives addictions, breaks up families, and corrupts the Church. If Christians cannot have demons, we must explain how hundreds of thousands of professed Christians are being delivered from demons with miraculous results, and how the giants of theology and revival could be so mistaken. That is an uphill battle, and the scriptural evidence to make any such case is greatly wanting.

In the last three years, deliverance has made an unprecedented revival. It is being taught by major influencers, accepted in more Churches, embraced by thousands of Christians who have come to Christ since 2020, and being taken back to the streets. The Church is again at a crossroads. Will we make the same blunder as we have for the last four hundred years and resist the return of deliverance?

# ABOUT THE AUTHOR

David Miller serves as the Pastor of Church Tsidkenu's New Hampshire Campus and an Instructor at Fire Academy, an innovative training program specializing in evangelism, deliverance, and charismatic gifts. With extensive training from Art Montgomery and Bob Larson, David has participated in over 2,000 deliverances and exorcisms. A graduate in Biblical Studies from Regent University, he is now advancing his theological education in the Master of Divinity program at Gordon-Conwell Seminary. David currently resides in Pittsfield, NH.

# BIBLIOGRAPHY

Anderson, Allan. "Exorcism and the Conversion to African Pentecostalism." *Exchange* 35, no. 1 (January 2006): 116–33.

Augustine. *City of God*. Translated by Henry Bettenson. London:
Penguin Classics, 2003.

Blumhardt, Johann Christoph. *Jesus Is Victor!: Blumhardt's Battle
with the Powers of Darkness*. Ebersbach an der Fils, Germany:
AwakenMedia, 2020.

Butler, Alban, Rev. "On the Writings of St. John Chrysostom."
*The Lives of the Fathers, Martyrs, and Other Principal Saints*.
Vol. I. Dublin: James Duffy, 1866; Bartleby.com, 2010.
https://www.bartleby.com/210/1/272.html.

Eusebius. *The History of the Church*. Edited by Andrew Louth.
Translated by G. A. Williamson. London: Penguin Classics,
1989.

Fernando, Ajith. *The NIV Application Commentary: Acts*. Grand
Rapids, MI: Zondervan, 1998.

Hammond, Frank, and Ida Mae Hammond. *Pigs in the Parlor: A Practical Guide to Deliverance*. Kirkwood, Mo: Impact Books, 1973.

Henry, Matthew. *Matthew Henry's Commentary on the Whole Bible: Complete and Unabridged*. Vol. 5. Peabody, MA: Hendrickson Publishers, 1991.

Jansons, Linards. "Baptismal Exorcism: An Exorcise in Liturgical Theology." *Lutheran Theological Journal* 45, no. 3 (December 2011): 183–97.

Kidd, Thomas S. "The Healing of Mercy Wheeler: Illness and Miracles among Early American Evangelicals." *William and Mary Quarterly* 63, no. 1 (January 1, 2006): 149–70. https://doi.org/10.2307/3491729.

Larson, Bob. *Curse Breaking*. Shippensburg, PA: Destiny Image, 2013.

Larson, Bob. *Dealing with Demons*. Shippensburg, PA: Destiny Image, 2016.

Larson, Bob. *Larson's Book of Spiritual Warfare*. Nashville, TN: Thomas Nelson, 1999.

Liardon, Roberts. *God's Generals: The Healing Evangelists*. New Kensington, PA: Whitaker House, 2011.

Liardon, Roberts. *God's Generals: The Revivalists*. New Kensington, PA: Whitaker House, 2008.

Liardon, Roberts. *God's Generals: The Roaring Reformers*. New Kensington, PA: Whitaker House, 2003.

Liardon, Roberts. *God's Generals: Why They Succeeded and Why Some Failed*. New Kensington, PA: Whitaker House, 1996.

MacMullen, Ramsay. *Christianizing the Roman Empire: A.D. 100–400*. New Haven, CT: Yale University Press, 1986.

Marshall, I. Howard. *The Acts of the Apostles: An Introduction and Commentary*. Grand Rapids, MI: William B. Eerdmans Publishing Company, 1980.

Mather, Cotton. *Memorable Providences*. Gale Ecco, Sabin Americana, 2012.

Mather, Cotton. *Wonders of the Invisible World. Observations as Well Historical as Theological, upon the Nature, the Number and the Operations of the Devils (1693)*. Edited by Reiner Smolinski. Lincoln, NE: University of Nebraska-Lincoln, n.d.

Murphy, Ed. *The Handbook for Spiritual Warfare*. Rev. ed. Nashville, TN: Thomas Nelson, 1996.

Nischan, Bodo. "The Exorcism Controversy and Baptism in the Late Reformation." *Sixteenth Century Journal* 18, no. 1 (1987). https://doi.org/10.2307/2540628.

Olson, Roger E. *The Story of Christian Theology*. Downers Grove, IL: IVP Academic, 1999.

Prince, Derek. *They Shall Expel Demons: What You Need to Know about Demons—Your Invisible Enemy*. Grand Rapids, MI: Chosen Books, 1998.

Shelley, Bruce L. *Church History in Plain Language*. 4th ed. Nashville, TN: Thomas Nelson, 2013.

Toner, Patrick. "Exorcist." In *The Catholic Encyclopedia*. Vol. 5. New York: Robert Appleton Company, 1909. https://www.newadvent.org/cathen/05711a.htm.

Twelftree, Graham H. *In the Name of Jesus: Exorcism among Early Christians*. Grand Rapids, MI: Baker Academic, 2007.

Welchel, Tommy, J. Edward Morris, and Cindy McCowan. *Azusa Street: They Told Me Their Stories: The Youth and Chil-*

*dren of Azusa Street Tell Their Stories*. Mustang, Oklahoma: Dare2Dream Books, 2006.

Wiersbe, Warren W. *The Bible Exposition Commentary: New Testament*. 2nd ed. Vol. 1. Colorado Springs, CO: David C. Cook, 2008.

Wigglesworth, Smith. *Ever Increasing Faith*. Rev ed. Springfield, MI: Gospel Publishing House, 1971.

Worley, Win. *Battling the Hosts of Hell*. Mesquite, TX: WRW Publications, 1976.

Worley, Win. *Warfare Prayers*. Mesquite, TX: WRW Publications, 2013.

Young, Francis. *A History of Exorcism in Catholic Christianity*. Cambridge: Palgrave Macmillan, 2016.

# A free ebook edition is available with the purchase of this book.

**To claim your free ebook edition:**

1. Visit MorganJamesBOGO.com
2. Sign your name CLEARLY in the space
3. Complete the form and submit a photo of the entire copyright page
4. You or your friend can download the ebook to your preferred device

**Morgan James BOGO™**

A **FREE** ebook edition is available for you or a friend with the purchase of this print book.

CLEARLY SIGN YOUR NAME ABOVE

**Instructions to claim your free ebook edition:**
1. Visit MorganJamesBOGO.com
2. Sign your name CLEARLY in the space above
3. Complete the form and submit a photo of this entire page
4. You or your friend can download the ebook to your preferred device

## Print & Digital Together Forever.

Snap a photo

Free ebook

Read anywhere

Printed in the USA
CPSIA information can be obtained
at www.ICGtesting.com
JSHW021520010824
67425JS00014B/106